Touch**Develop**

Programming
on the Go

T0219530

Touch**Develop**

Programming
on the Go

R Nigel Horspool

University of Victoria

Nikolai Tillmann

Microsoft Research

Microsoft Research

TouchDevelop: Programming on the Go
by R. Nigel Horspool and Nikolai Tillmann
Copyright © 2013 by Apress Media, LLC, all rights reserved.

President and Publisher: Paul Manning
Editor: Jeffrey Pepper

Distributed to the book trade worldwide by Springer Science+Business Media New York, 233 Spring Street, 6th Floor, New York, NY 10013. Phone 1-800-SPRINGER, fax (201) 348-4505, e-mail orders-ny@springer-sbm.com, or visit www.springeronline.com. For information on translations, please e-mail rights@apress.com, or visit www.apress.com.

Contents

Preface

The sales figures for smartphones continue to rise exponentially. Tablet computers are showing a similarly phenomenal adoption rate and are replacing laptop computers in many areas of life. We can imagine a time when nearly everyone is carrying around a powerful computer in the form of a smartphone or a tablet. The term *mobile device* is used to cover such devices. Typically, an *app* (an application program) for a smartphone or tablet has to be developed in a PC and transferred to the mobile device later. But does it have to be that way? The TouchDevelop project at Microsoft Research has proved that the answer is No. TouchDevelop is a programming environment that runs on all mobile devices. It allows a script to be developed on a mobile device, or on a PC, and to be run on any mobile device or a PC. After releasing the app in 2011 when it was available only for the Windows Phone, the overwhelming response was a big surprised us: more than 200,000 users downloaded the app and they published more than 10,000 scripts written entirely on phones. Since then, TouchDevelop has been made available in a form that runs on PC, Mac and Linux platforms, and on iPad, iPhone, iPod Touch and Android devices. TouchDevelop is truly a portable development environment for creating portable apps.

Who this book is for

Mobile devices represent the latest in technology. Furthermore, many students actually own their own smartphone. High school teachers and college or university instructors love the idea of using the latest technology to engage their students. While they may be experts in the field of teaching programming, many teachers appreciate guidance on how to navigate a complex app like TouchDevelop: its visual program editor is designed for touchscreens and uses different editing paradigms from a traditional keyboard-based text processor. Another opportunity and challenge is how to make use of some of the sensors that a modern mobile device has to offer.

This book has much to offer to both both teachers and self-starting students who are learning how to program on their own. For teachers, it walks in detail through all of the screens of the app, and it points out similarities and differences of the TouchDevelop language compared to other programming languages that the teacher might already be familiar with. For students and enthusiasts, the book can serve as a handy reference which they keep next to the device they are using – it is particularly useful when that device has a small screen. The book systematically addresses all programming language constructs, starting from the very basic constructs such as variables and loops. The book also explores many of the phone sensors and data sources which make creating apps for mobile devices so rewarding.

If you are new to programming with TouchDevelop, or if you have not yet worked on touchscreen devices, we suggest that you read the book starting from Chapter 1. If you are already familiar with the basic paradigm of the TouchDevelop programming environment, then feel free to jump ahead to the later chapters that address particular topic areas.

This book is written from the perspective of a person developing their code using a browser. All screenshots and navigation instructions refer to the TouchDevelop Web App running in a browser and is applicable to all platforms except the Windows Phone. Only Appendix E, which covers the editor on the Windows Phone, uses screenshots and instructions specific to the Windows Phone.

This book is available online as well as being publish in print form by APress. Please email touchdevelop@microsoft.com to give feedback.

Background to the book

This edition of the book is the result of the year-long evolution of earlier book versions, incorporating feedback from tutorials and lectures given by the authors. The first version of the book was produced as limited edition of 75 copies for the ACM SIGCSE Conference in Raleigh, NC, March, 2012. That book was based on the recently released Version 2.6 of TouchDevelop. An updated copy of the book with 1000 copies, based on Version 2.10, was printed in January 2013. This book was made available via a Creative Commons Licence and put on the Amazon Bookstore as well as the TouchDevelop website. Much of the contents of the second book were also applicable to the Web App version of TouchDevelop, though all the screenshots were still of a phone. This third version has been retargeted at the Web App version of TouchDevelop.

Other learning materials

On the TouchDevelop website, you can also find extensive videos, tutorials and slides to help you learn and teach TouchDevelop. Just tap (or click) on the large tile labeled "Docs" under the "Chat and Learn" heading once you have logged in to the TouchDevelop website to find these learning resources.

Comments are very welcome. To contact the TouchDevelop team or the authors, you can

- Send email to touchdevelop@microsoft.com
- Post on https://facebook.com/touchdevelop
- Post on the forum in the app

Acknowledgments

As the TouchDevelop community grows, we are finding that we are learning from everyone who engages in the project – students at Hackathons, academics who write papers, and most of all developers of the amazing apps in the bazaar. Thanks to all of you.

Important websites

https://www.touchdevelop.com
https://www.facebook.com/TouchDevelop
http://research.microsoft.com/touchdevelop

The TouchDevelop Team

 **Thomas (Tom) Ball** is a principal researcher and research manager at Microsoft Research, Redmond, widely known for his work in program profiling, software model checking, program testing, and empirical software engineering. Ball is a 2011 ACM Fellow for "contributions to software analysis and defect detection." Since becoming a manager at Microsoft, he has nurtured and grown research areas such as automated theorem proving, program testing and verification, and empirical software engineering. He

holds a B.A. in Computer Science from Cornell University and a M.S. and Ph.D. from the University of Wisconsin-Madison.

Judith Bishop is Director of Computer Science at Microsoft Research, based in Redmond, USA. Her role is to create strong links between Microsoft's research groups and universities globally, through encouraging projects, supporting conferences and engaging directly in research. Her expertise is in programming languages and distributed systems, with a strong practical bias and an interest in compilers and design patterns. She is the author or editor of 17 books on programming languages. She has a PhD from the University of Southampton, UK in Computer Science.

Sebastian Burckhardt is a Researcher at Microsoft Research. He was born and raised in Basel, Switzerland. His research interests revolve around the general problem of programming concurrent, parallel, and distributed systems conveniently, efficiently, and correctly. More specific interests include consistency models, concurrency testing, self-adjusting computation, and the concurrent revisions programming model. After a few years of industry experience at IBM, he earned his PhD in Computer Science at the University of Pennsylvania.

Juan Chen is a Researcher in the RiSE group at Microsoft Research Redmond. Her main research areas include compilers, programming verification, and type systems. She has worked on certifying compilers for object-oriented languages, and design and implementation of a functional programming language for specifying and verifying program properties. She has a PhD in Computer Science from Princeton University.

Jonathan 'Peli' de Halleux is a Software Engineer in the Research in Software Engineering group at Microsoft Research. Peli also volunteers at the local high school to teach mobile computer science. From 2004 to 2006, he worked in the Common Language Runtime (CLR) as a Software Design Engineer in Test in charge of the Just In Time compiler. He has a PhD in Applied Mathematics from the Catholic University of Louvain, Belgium.

Manuel Fähndrich is a Senior Researcher in the RiSE group at Microsoft Research in Redmond. He works on programming language design, static type systems, program analysis and verification, as well as runtime techniques and optimizations. His past and current project involvements include the Singularity OS and Sing# language, CodeContracts for .NET, and TouchDevelop. He has a PhD from the University of California, Berkeley.

Nigel Horspool is a professor of computer science at the University of Victoria. His main focus for research and teaching has been programming languages and compilers, though his main claim to fame is a string searching algorithm. He is the author or co-author of three books, which cover the C language, Unix and the C# language. He is currently the co-editor of the journal 'Software: Practice and Experience'. He has a PhD from the University of Toronto, Canada in Computer Science.

Michał Moskal is a Researcher in Redmond. He is in the RiSE group working on software verification, automated theorem proving, and programming languages. He works on a formal verifier for concurrent C programs called VCC, while also taking on other projects including Boogie intermediate verification language, SPUR tracing JIT, and DKAL authorization engine. He has a PhD from the University of Wrocław, Poland.

Arjmand Samuel works with the academic community to foster research and collaborations in the devices and services research areas. He leads the mobile and cloud computing research and outreach for Microsoft Research (Project Hawaii and TouchDevelop). His recent research interests are in software architectures and programming paradigms for devices of all shapes and forms (TouchDevelop and HomeOS). He has published in a variety of publications on topics of security, privacy, location aware access control, and innovative use of mobile technology. Samuel has a Ph.D. in Information Security from Purdue University.

Nikolai Tillmann is a Principal Research Software Design Engineer, Microsoft Research. His main areas of research are program authoring on mobile devices, program analysis, testing, optimization, and verification. He started the TouchDevelop project, which enables end-users to write programs for mobile devices on mobile devices. He also leads the Pex project, in which he develops together with Peli de Halleux a framework for runtime verification and automatic test case generation for .NET applications based on parameterized unit testing and dynamic symbolic execution. Nikolai has a Dipl. Inf. in Computer Science from TU Berlin, Germany.

List of figures

List of tables

Chapter 1
Introduction to TouchDevelop

TouchDevelop is a complete app creation ecosystem designed for touch, cloud connected, mobile devices. This chapter provides a brief introduction to the world of TouchDevelop scripting and the devices that support it.

1.1 Computers want to be programmed

Computers are everywhere, and they take on many different forms: TVs, smart phones, fridges with apps, etc. Despite this abundance of form and function, until recently, most people thought of desktop PCs and then laptops when they were asked about computers. This perception is shifting, as smartphones and tablets are quickly becoming the main computers for an increasing number of people. As a matter of fact, smartphone sales have surpassed PC sales even faster than some analysts anticipated.

New smartphone and tablet models are getting more powerful and becoming suitable for many tasks that used to require PCs. Mobile devices have become well established tools for reading and composing emails, browsing the web, and playing games. These devices are even being used to annotate documents. And yet, the one task that can be seen as the defining moment of any computing platform is not yet widely performed on smartphones and tablets: writing code, or even creating entire applications.

The previous generation of people who grew up with full featured PCs always had the option to program them. While most people chose not to do that, they at least had the option. Decades of programming language and development environment research produced powerful tools suitable for PCs. It is through exploring this opportunity that many young people became interested in computer science.

Unfortunately, in the new world of apps and app marketplaces with a focus on existing curated content, it seems that the creative outlet of programming that encouraged aspiring programmers in the past is no longer easily accessible. The ability to program on the very device one owns and uses all the time is not a prominent option anymore.

Granted, smartphones and tablets pose new challenges for programming tasks. These devices have no physical keyboard, the screen tends to be rather small, and data tends to not be stored locally but is dynamically fetched from the cloud. A group at Microsoft Research asked the question: "Is it possible to create interesting apps directly on a smartphone, without using a separate PC or a keyboard?" It is in the attempt to answer this question that TouchDevelop was born.

The TouchDevelop team took on the challenge of rethinking computer programming from the ground up, trying to understand how a modern mobile touch-screen device should be programmed in its own right. TouchDevelop was created with a goal to ignore the legacy of programming languages optimized for linear text input via a keyboard, often having a verbosity that assumes big screens.

We believe that as more people adopt mobile devices as their primary, or possibly only, computing devices, it will become more important to not just enable users to consume content but to also empower them to produce content. We particularly believe in empowering users to produce new applications.

1.2   What is TouchDevelop?

TouchDevelop is a novel application development environment that allows anyone to script their mobile devices anywhere. It does not need a separate

PC and can be used by students, hobbyists, power users, and developers. Through TouchDevelop, users can create scripts (i.e., apps written using TouchDevelop) to access data, media, and sensors on a smart phone, tablet or PC. The scripts can also interact with the cloud services for storage, computing, and social networks. TouchDevelop applications can serve many purposes and are typically written for fun, for personalizing the phone, and for creating productivity tools.

TouchDevelop brings the excitement of the first programmable personal computers to the now ubiquitous mobile devices. Scripts developed using TouchDevelop allow users to show and manipulate music and pictures stored on their own mobile devices, to use the device's sensors, and to interact with friends in their social networks.

TouchDevelop can be used to develop games such as "missile defense", which is a full featured game where cities must be defended against incoming missiles (https://www.touchdevelop.com/zvpj). The script for this sample game can be downloaded to the TouchDevelop application installed on a Windows Phone or directly from the TouchDevelop web application. The user has full access to the script and can modify the game in any way imaginable. If someone has made improvements to the game, the improved game can be shared with others. It is as simple as tapping a button to upload the changed script back to the website. The script will be assigned a different identification tag (replacing the /zvpj letters at the end of the URL). If the author of missile defense publishes an update, TouchDevelop will automatically redirect the user to the latest version of that game.

An example of a TouchDevelop script being used for productivity is the "my online meetings" script, which finds active online meetings. If there is one, it can be joined through the Microsoft Lync application installed on the phone (https://www.touchdevelop.com/mpuj).

The TouchDevelop website provides a variety of scripts that can be used for learning or as examples. Sample scripts meant to illustrate how to use the built-in APIs can be found at the URL https://www.touchdevelop.com/pboj. Scripts written by other users can be found by going to the TouchDevelop URL https://www.touchdevelop.com/search and entering a term like 'game' into the search box. Alternatively one can explore the on-line API manual at https://www.touchdevelop.com/doc/api.

1.3   The TouchDevelop ecosystem

A script developed using the TouchDevelop editor can be shared with other users by using the TouchDevelop cloud infrastructure at https://www.touchdevelop.com.

Figure 1-1 gives a high level architectural overview of the TouchDevelop ecosystem: regardless of whether a phone or browser client is used, all information such as scripts is retrieved and stored in the touchdevelop.com cloud service.

Figure 1-1: The TouchDevelop ecosystem

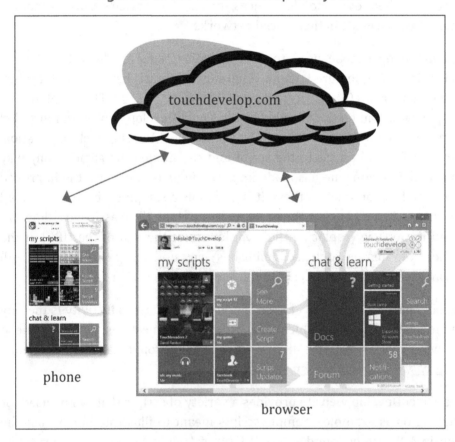

TouchDevelop scripts are developed by users on their devices and executed within the TouchDevelop run time environment. These scripts can be shared with other users. The TouchDevelop cloud infrastructure supports this sharing amongst a community of TouchDevelop users. These scripts can also be searched, viewed, and installed into a user's account using the TouchDevelop website. The cloud infrastructure enables sharing, and, acts as a repository of all scripts developed and published by users.

The TouchDevelop website allocates a unique deep link for each script on http://touchdevelop.com; where each script is identified by a seemingly random letter sequence. For example, https://www.touchdevelop.com/zpco refers to a particular version of the TouchInvaders game, as in Figure 1-2. It can be used to open the script directly. This link can be shared with other people or on social networks.

Figure 1-2: Viewing metadata of a script

If a user likes this script, he or she can show their appreciation of a script or a comment by giving it a positive review in the form of a "heart".

On any client, a phone or a web browser, the user can edit a script as shown in Figure 1-3.

Figure 1-3: Editing a script

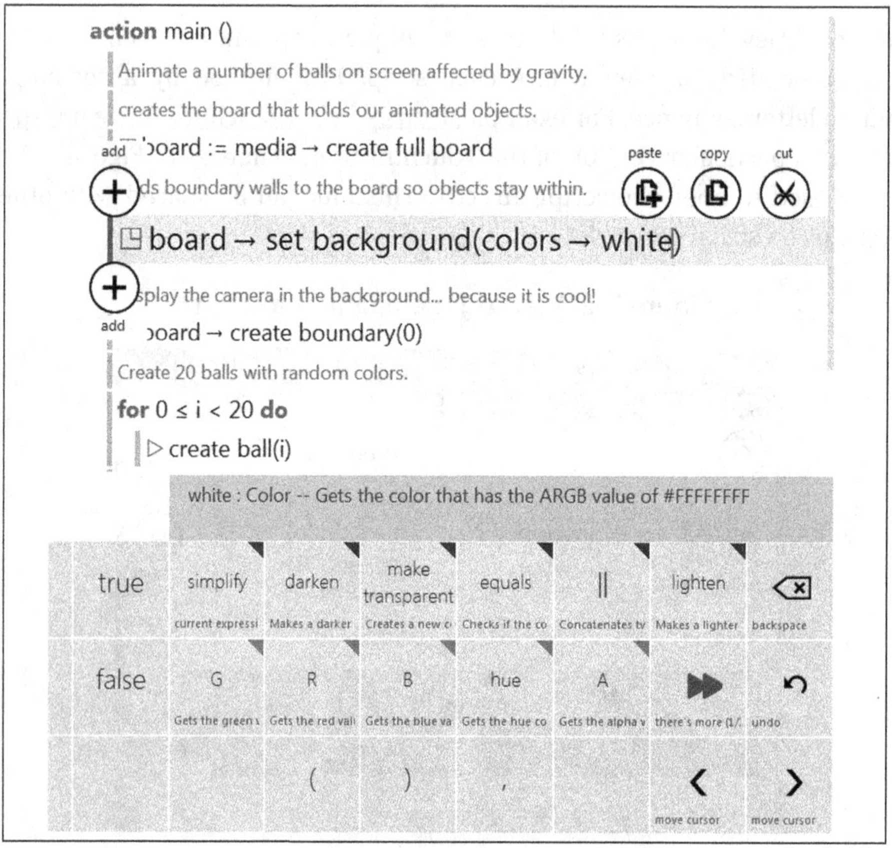

1.4   History and Future

After releasing TouchDevelop in April of 2011, first exclusively available for Windows Phone, the overwhelming response surprised us. Since then, more than 300,000 people downloaded the app. At first, TouchDevelop was limited to creating scripts on the device where it was installed – there was no way to share scripts with other people.

In August 2011, the update to v2.0 of TouchDevelop brought sharing of scripts via the touchdevelop.com cloud service. The update also enabled many more social features such as reviewing scripts, writing comments, taking screenshots, etc. Since then, more than 90,000 people registered online and shared more than 25,000 scripts, most of them written entirely on phones. Many features were added over time, making TouchDevelop an increasingly powerful development environment and language. The features include support for libraries for code reuse and custom structured data types.

In order to share scripts not only within the TouchDevelop environment, but also with other people who might not be aware of TouchDevelop, we added the ability to export scripts as apps that can be submitted to the Windows Phone Store. This capability has existed since March of 2012.

In October 2012, TouchDevelop took a giant step forward. Thanks to a complete re-implementation, TouchDevelop could now run not just on Windows Phones, but on virtually any modern device in a browser as a Web App. The supported platforms include PC, Mac, iPhone, iPad, iPod Touch, and Android. The new TouchDevelop implementation harnesses the power of HTML5 and JavaScript, while still using the same programming language as before. The code editor dynamically adjusts to the screen size to accommodate small screens on smartphones, medium-sized screens on tablets, and large screens on PCs. The user interface of the Web App has again been optimized for touchscreens, but a keyboard and a mouse can also be used if desired and available. At the same time, we also added the ability to export scripts as apps that can be submitted to the Windows Store (which is a separate concern from the Windows Phone Store).

In the near future, the update v3.0 of the TouchDevelop app for Windows Phone will bring the same editing and execution engine that currently powers the TouchDevelop Web App to Windows Phone 8 devices.

A significant upcoming addition to the TouchDevelop programming language will be the concept of "cloud state." By just tagging a variable as "cloud", similar to how one marks a variable as "static" in C#, an app is turned into a distributed app with shared state. All changes to that variable will get automatically synchronized between different devices and users.

1.5   Platforms

There are a number of optional sensors for Windows Phones. "Near field communication" (NFC), front camera, rear camera, magnetometer and gyroscope may or may not be present in any given device model. Similarly, some browsers choose to expose certain sensors while others don't. Safari on iOS exposes the accelerometer; Chrome on Android only partially, and Internet Explorer 10 not at all. This variety is most likely an artifact of the continuously evolving HTML5 standard; so, hopefully, more and more sensors will be supported by all browsers as time goes by.

Depending on these constraints, and depending on whether you are running the native TouchDevelop app on Windows Phone or the Web App in the browser, different feature sets are available to you when you write your scripts. See https://www.touchdevelop.com/platforms for a complete and up-to-date overview of the different platform capabilities.

1.5.1   Installing TouchDevelop on a Windows phone

If TouchDevelop is to be used for the first time on a Windows Phone, it will need to be installed. To install the app, follow these steps:

1. Tap the Store tile on the Windows phone.
2. Press the search icon at the bottom of the screen, and type the text 'touchdevelop' into the Store Search text box. Before you finish typing all the letters, the TouchDevelop app should appear as a choice on the screen.
3. Tap that choice to select it.
4. Tap Install.

If your device is running a Windows Phone 7 or 7.5 or 7.8 operating system, then you will get TouchDevelop v2.0, which uses a slightly different user interface that does not match the screenshots in this book, and its language is a subset what is discussed in this book.

If your device is running Windows Phone 8, then you will get TouchDevelop v3.0, which resembles the Web App at https://www.touchdevelop.com/app, but it exposes many more sensors and data providers available on the phone.

1.5.2   Running TouchDevelop on other platforms

On all other platforms, TouchDevelop does not come as an app in a marketplace, but instead as a Web App. You can run it from your web browser:

1. Go to https://www.touchdevelop.com/
2. Log in. You will be taken to the Web App.

1.6   The scripting language

TouchDevelop is a language for writing mobile apps. The TouchDevelop Windows Phone application and the web app also provide a runtime environment for executing TouchDevelop scripts.

The TouchDevelop language is a typed, structured programming language built around the idea of only using touch to author code. It has built-in primitives that make it easy to access the rich sensor data available on a mobile device. The TouchDevelop language mixes imperative, object-oriented, and functional features. The imperative parts are the most visible: users can update local variables, and the states of global objects. Object-orientation is dictated by auto completion requirements – properties of objects are an easily accessible and intuitive concept. However, for the sake of simplicity, the language does not provide the ability to define new types which are subtypes of other types.

A TouchDevelop script consists of a number of actions (functions or procedures), events (actions to be performed when an external event occurs), definitions of tables and record types, global state (global variables and read-only data) and library references (references to other scripts). The language is covered in some depth in Chapter 2.

The TouchDevelop script editor is part of the TouchDevelop application. It is designed for efficient entry of scripts using only the touchscreen. TouchDevelop scripts execute within the TouchDevelop application. The mode of execution is entirely reactive - actions are run in response to events. Events can be raised by user input (e.g., interacting with a UI element, changing the orientation of the phone, or shaking it), events from the phone (e.g., change of active song in the song player) or passage of time. TouchDevelop uses cooperative multi-threading. Actions and events are executed in a single-threaded manner.

Chapter 2
The Scripting Language

A TouchDevelop script appears to the user as statements in a language which is not unlike many other programming languages. This chapter covers the syntax and semantics of that language. The language is augmented by a powerful and rich API (Application Programming Interface), an API which significantly extends the programming capabilities of the TouchDevelop language. The API is covered in the chapters which follow this one.

2.1   Introduction – the language flavor

These introductory paragraphs are written for people who know some of the terminology used to describe programming language semantics, and will allow such readers to fast forward over large chunks of this chapter.

The scripting language is statement oriented. Statements are executed in a *sequential* manner. Control flow constructs include *if*-statements, *for* and *while* loops, and *functions* (which are called *actions* in this language).

The statements manipulate values. All intermediate values and variables are *statically type checked*. Only parameters of actions have explicit type declarations. The datatypes of all other values and variables are inferred through analysis of the code.

The language is *strongly typed*, in that (with one exception), every operation requires operands of particular datatypes and there is *no automatic coercion* to the type required by an operation. The datatypes belong to one of two categories: *value types* and *reference types*. Value types may have storage on the *stack* used for local variables, and their storage is automatically deallocated on exit from an action (i.e. from a function). Reference types have their storage allocated on the *heap*.

The heap is garbage collected. In addition to parameters and local variables, a script can define globally visible variables in its data section or read-only variables in its art section. Their storage is persistent across script executions.

Although the language syntax shows similarities to object-oriented languages, the language does not support the object-oriented paradigm. For example, there is no equivalent of class inheritance or method overloading.

To conserve real estate on smaller screens, several symbols are used instead of keywords. These symbols are all available as characters in the Segoe UI Symbol font (a font which is distributed with the Windows 7 and 8 operating systems). The symbols are summarized in Table 2-1.

2.1.1   A sample program (/okzc)

This sample program is shown in Figure 2-1. It uses several features provided by the API. They will be explained only briefly. More complete explanations are provided in later chapters. Note that this script runs only on a Windows Phone.

The script comprises two actions and two events. The action named main is the entry point for the script. The action named display song is called by main. It has one input parameter named song (with type Song) and has one result parameter named result (with type Number).

The main action defines and initializes a local variable named found. No datatype is provided in that definition; it is inferred from the value used for initialization which has type Number. The local variable named songs is, by using the API, initialized with a collection of all songs held on the phone.

Table 2-1: Special symbols used in scripts

Symbol	Unicode Value	Description
→	U+2192	Select a method or field belonging to the value provided on the left
▷	U+25B7	Call the action named on the right and defined in the current script
⌗	U+25F3	Access a global persistent variable defined in the data section of the script
△	U+267B	Call a function defined in another script, which has been published as a library
⌸	U+2339	Access a datatype or item declared in the record section of the script
✿	U+273F	Access a value in the art section of the script

A **for-each** loop steps through every value in the collection, assigning the next variable to a new local variable named song. The first statement inside the loop calls an action using the notation ▷display song(song). It passes a reference to the local variable song and receives a number back as the result, adding that to the found variable.

The second statement inside the loop takes a string constant and concatenates the value of the global data item named played. The preceding symbol ⌗ indicates that the variable has global scope and is persistent. The string concatenation operator is ‖ and is the only operator in TouchDevelop which is overloaded – meaning that it accepts operands with any datatypes and those operand values are converted to strings.

The resulting string value constructed by the concatenation appears to the left of the arrow operator →. It indicates that the value is to be transmitted to the method shown on the right, whose name is post to wall. Almost every datatype has a post to wall method; it causes a representation of the value to be displayed on the screen.

The sample script contains two events. An *event* is an action which is executed whenever the specified event occurs. The shake event is caused by physically shaking the phone. When shaking is detected by the phone's sensors, the code provided for the shake event is executed. Events do not interrupt each other; they are executed in first-come first-served order.

Figure 2-1: The 'new songs' script (/okzc)

```
action main ( )
    // Finds songs not played yet.
    var found := 0
    var songs := media → songs
    for each song in songs where true
    do
        found := found + ▷ display song(song)
    ("Songs played with this app: " ‖ ⊞ played) → post to wall
    ("Songs never played: " ‖ found) → post to wall

private action display song ( song : Song ) returns ( result : Number )
do
    // Post a song to the wall if not played yet and returns 1
    // otherwise returns 1.
    if song → play count = 0 then
        song → post to wall
        result := 1
    else
        result := 0

event active song changed ( )
    // Increment song played counter.
    ⊞ played := ⊞ played + 1

event shake ( )
    // Pauses and resume playing.
    if player → is playing then
        player → pause
    else
        player → resume

data played : Number
```

If a script contains one or more events, the main program does not terminate. It waits for events to occur. In this case, the script terminates only if halted by the user (e.g. tapping the phone's back button) or if it executes a call to a method in the API for that purpose (time→stop).

2.2   Datatypes and variables

Each type (except the special type Nothing) belongs to one of two categories: *Value Types* or *Reference Types*. If a variable has a value type, then storage for an instance of that type is held inside the variable itself. For example, a variable with type Number is allocated storage which is used to hold number values. However, if a variable has a reference type, then storage for its value is allocated on the heap and the variable holds a reference to that heap storage.

2.2.1   The Invalid value

Every datatype (except the special type Nothing) has a special value Invalid in addition to all its normal values. This special value is normally used to indicate that a global data variable has not been initialized or that a method in the API was unable to return a value. TouchDevelop provides a method for testing a value of any datatype (except Nothing) to test whether it is the Invalid value. There are also API methods for obtaining the Invalid value for any desired type.

If a data structure (such as a tree or linked list) is constructed using Object types declared in the Records section of a script, the Invalid value would usually be used to play the role of a null reference value.

Some code to demonstrate the use of Invalid values appears below.

```
var numUsers := 0
...
if connection failure detected then
    numUsers := invalid → number
else

...
if numUsers → is invalid then
    "Script is terminating" → post to wall
else
```

2.2.2   The Nothing type

A method or an operation which does not return a usable result, but which otherwise succeeded, actually returns a value of type Nothing. For example, the post to wall method which is provided for every datatype returns a result of type Nothing. In some languages, such as F#, the Unit type is the equivalent of the Nothing type in TouchDevelop. There is a single value with type Nothing. No operations at all are provided for this type; it is similar to the void type in languages like C/C++ and Java.

Value types

The basic types or elementary types provided in the TouchDevelop scripting language are Number, Boolean, and String. These are all *Value Types*. There are also several composite types which are value types. All the value types are listed in Table 2-2. Here are some further details about the Number and String types.

Number

The Number type combines the integer and floating-point types found in other languages. Values are held in double-precision floating point format, consistent with the IEEE 754 standard. This implies that the special values *plus infinity*, *minus infinity* and *NaN* (not-a-number) can be computed as the result of a calculation.

When a Number value is used in a context where an integer is needed, such as when selecting the k-th value in a collection, the value is rounded to the closest integer. A value exactly half-way between is rounded up; for example, 1.5 is rounded up to 2 while 1.49 is rounded down to 1.

Table 2-2: The Value types

Value Type	Description	Covered in Chapter
Number	An integer or floating-point number	2
Boolean	The type whose constants are true and false	2
String	A sequence of zero or more Unicode characters	2
Color	Used for colors displayed on the screen. Values are compatible with 4 byte ARGB (alpha, red, green, blue) color representations. Many standard colors are provided as constants of the Color datatype.	6

Value Type	Description	Covered in Chapter
DateTime	Holds any date from 0001 CE (Common Era) to 9999 CE, combined with a time of day. The time of day is recorded with 100 nanosecond accuracy.	8
Location	Holds a combination of latitude, longitude and altitude values plus a course direction and a speed in two-dimensional space.	8
Motion	A combination of sensor readings which describe motion of the phone in 3D space plus a time-stamp which specifies when the readings were taken. The motion information includes speed, acceleration and angular velocity.	7
Vector3	A triple of three numbers used to hold a velocity or acceleration in the three spatial dimensions or an angular velocity about the three axes in 3D space.	7

String

A string may contain zero or more Unicode characters. When a string constant is shown as part of a TouchDevelop script, double-quote characters are used to enclose the string and a backslash character is used to escape a double-quote character or a special character which appears inside the string. However, when using the editor to enter a string constant, no backslash characters should be entered (unless a backslash character itself is wanted inside the string constant).

It should be noted that TouchDevelop does not provide the char type for working with single characters. Instead a string of length one should be used.

2.2.3   Reference types

Storage for an instance of a reference type is allocated in a different place from a variable declared with that type. A local variable with a reference type is implemented as a pointer (a reference) to the actual value which is stored elsewhere.

In TouchDevelop, two kinds of reference types are provided. If the value represents an entity which exists outside TouchDevelop, such as a song on a Windows phone, then storage is allocated outside the TouchDevelop application. Otherwise the storage is allocated within an area of memory controlled by TouchDevelop which is called the *heap*. When there are no more references to a value on the heap, the storage used by that value is automatically reclaimed. It is *garbage collected*. The language facilities and the operations which can be performed on reference types in a TouchDevelop script depend on whether the values are external to the script or are internal.

When one variable with a reference type is assigned to another variable, both variables will become references to the same instance. A simple example to illustrate this sharing of one instance between two variables is provided by the following code.

```
// Set x to refer to a value of type Contact
var x := social → choose contacts
var y := x
x → set title("His Excellency")
y → title → post to wall
```

In this example, the title displayed on the screen by the last statement will always be 'His Excellency' because x and y are both references to the same instance on the heap, in which the title field of an instance of the Contact type has been set to that string.

Reference types provided by the API

Excluding the collection types (which are covered in the next subsection of this chapter below), Table 2-3 lists the reference types implemented by the API and available to TouchDevelop scripts. The table explicitly indicates whether storage for an instance of each type is allocated on the heap or is external to the TouchDevelop script.

Table 2-3: Reference types provided by the API

Reference Type	Description	Storage	Covered in Chapter
Appointment	A calendar appointment	Heap	8
Board	A 2D canvas on which sprites can be drawn and moved	Heap	9
Camera	The front or back camera	External	6

Reference Type	Description	Storage	Covered in Chapter
Contact	Contact information and details about a person or company	External	8
Form Builder	Used to create HTML form data	Heap	--
Json Builder	A JSON data structure builder	Heap	--
Json Object	A JSON data structure (obtained from a website)	Heap	4
Link	A link to a video, image, e-mail or phone number	Heap	5,6,8
Location	A geographic location	Heap	7,8
Map	A BING map	Heap	8
Matrix	a 2-D matrix of numbers	Heap	--
Media Link	A media file on the home network	External	5,6
Message	A posting on a message board	Heap	8
OAuth Response	OAuth 2.0 access token or error	Heap	11
Page	A page on the wall	Heap	3
Page Button	A button on the wall which can be tapped	Heap	3
Picture	A rectangular picture containing graphics or a photograph	External	6
Picture Album	A named album of pictures	External	6
Place	A named location	Heap	8
Playlist	A song playlist	Heap	5
Song	A song	External	5
Song Album	A song album	External	5
Sound	A sound clip	Heap	5
Sprite	A graphical object which can be displayed on a Board instance	Heap	9
TextBox	A box used to display text on the screen	Heap	6
Web Request	A HTTP web request	Heap	4
Web Response	A HTTP web response	Heap	4
Xml Object	A XML element or collection of elements	Heap	4

Collection types

The API also provides homogeneous collections. A collection contains zero or more elements whose type is one of the value types or one of the reference types listed in Table 2-2. Collections are provided for many of the possible element types. When a collection type has not been provided, an equivalent list type can be defined instead using an *Object* declaration (see Objects and Decorators, below).

Some collections correspond to resources provided on a Windows Phone (and therefore may not be supported on other platforms), such as a collection of stored songs, and such collections are immutable. Other collections are mutable, meaning that new elements can be inserted into the collection and/or elements may be deleted.

The collection types provided by the API are listed in Table 2-4 and Table 2-5. Three of the collection types have been tagged as special and are listed separately in Table 2-5. These three collection types have some special properties not possessed by the other collection types and need some additional explanation.

2.2.4   Tables and indexes

The Records section of a TouchDevelop script can contain definitions of Tables. Each *Table type* is a datatype with a single instance and is globally visible. It corresponds to a database table which consists of rows and whose fields are organized into columns. The Records section can also contain definitions for Index types.

2.2.5   Objects

The Records section of a script can include declarations for Object types. Each Object type is a new datatype which is composed from named fields, similar to a struct or class type in other languages. Storage for instances of Object types is allocated on the heap and is garbage collected. Since it is heap allocated, every Object type is a *Reference type*.

Table 2-4: Regular collection types

Collection Type	Element Type	Mutable?	Covered in Chapter
Appointment Collection	Appointment	No	8
Contact Collection	Contact	No	8
Link Collection	Link	Yes	8
Location Collection	Location	Yes	7,8

Collection Type	Element Type	Mutable?	Covered in Chapter
Media Link Collection	Media Link	No	5,6
Message Collection	Message	Yes	8
Number Collection	Number	Yes	2
Page Collection	Page	No	3
Picture Albums	Picture Album	No	6
Pictures	Picture	No	6
Place Collection	Place	Yes	8
Playlists	Playlist	No	5
Song Albums	Song Album	No	5
Songs	Song	No	5
String Collection	String	Yes	2

Table 2-5: Special collection types

Collection Type	Element Type	Mutable?	Covered in Chapter
Number Map	Number	Yes	2
String Map	String	Yes	2
Sprite Set	Sprite	Yes	9

2.2.6   Decorators

Decorators may be declared in the Records section of a script. A decorator is used to associate extra information with instances of some reference types. The types which can be decorated are Appointment, Board, Json Object, Link, Map, Message, Page, Page Button, Place, Sound, Sprite, TextBox, Tile, Web Request, Web Response, Xml Object and Sprite Set. User-defined objects can be decorated as well.

2.2.7   Global persistent data

The Data section of a TouchDevelop script may contain declarations for global variables. Each of these variables has a datatype which must be one of the types provided in the language or API or one of the *Object* types declared in the Records section of the script.

Any global variable declared to have a simple type or the DateTime type is initialized to a neutral value. The neutral values are 0 for a Number, false for a Boolean, "" for a String, and 1/1/0001 12:00:00 AM for a DateTime variable. A variable with any other type is initialized to a special *invalid value.*

The is invalid method is provided for every datatype and may be used to test whether a global variable has not yet been initialized or a value was unobtainable. For example, if the Data section of the script contains a declaration for the global variable MyFriends with the type String Collection, then this script might contain statements like the following to check whether the variable needs to be initialized.

```
if ⊞MyFriends → is invalid then
    // it's the first use of this script, initialize the global variable
    ⊞MyFriends := collections → create string collection
else
    // do nothing
```

The values held by many of the global variables persist from one execution of the script to the next because they are held in the phone's memory. The only ways to 'forget' these values are to uninstall the script or edit the script and delete the global variables.

2.2.8   Art items

Some scripts need to display pictures or to produce sounds. These pictures or sounds can be added to the script as global constants and become part of the script. Such items are held in the Art section of the script. In addition, the Art section can contain definitions for particular colors which will be needed by the script.

The Art section of the script is similar to the Data section except that the items are restricted to having one of the datatypes Color, Picture or Sound, and these items are initialized. Initialization for a Color value is provided via an ARGB (alpha, red, green, blue) value; initialization for Picture or Sound values is obtained by downloading the desired value from a web site.

2.3   Expressions

2.3.1   Constants

Explicit constants of type Number, String and Boolean can be directly entered into scripts using the editor. Named constants with the types Color, Picture and Sound can also be incorporated into a script, but their values have to be specified through special mechanisms and these values are accessed through the use of entries in the Art section of a script. Finally, there is a special kind of constant, invalid, which is provided for every datatype.

Explicit Constants

Number constants are written in the usual formats for non-negative decimal integers and non-negative decimal fixed-point constants. The maximum value, minimum value and precision correspond to the IEEE 754 standard for 64 bit floating point numbers. Integers with magnitudes up to approximately 10^{14} are represented exactly. Larger values are subject to round-off error. These are some examples of valid Number constants.

   0   23   001   3.14159   100000.99

Note that it is not possible to write a negative numeric constant. Thus, the parentheses are necessary in the following statement.

   (- 3) → post to wall

The value being printed is an expression composed of the unary negation operator applied to the positive constant 3. If the parentheses are omitted, a semantic error is reported.

String constants can be entered with the TouchDevelop editor and can directly contain any characters provided on the keyboard. Although strings are implemented as sequences of Unicode characters, no mechanism is provided for including an arbitrary Unicode character in a string constant. (The full complement of Unicode characters is available only through the to character method of the Number type.) Some examples of String constants are as follows.

   "" "abc" "hello there"

The two Boolean constants can be entered directly using the editor. They appear in scripts as follows.

   true false

Named constants

The TouchDevelop WebApp editor provides a mechanism to add named constants of type Color Sound Picture String and Number to the **art** section of a script. Tapping the plus symbol below the *art* heading in the editor window and choosing Color as the type of the new resource brings up a window to select a new color. Four sliders allow the alpha, red, green and blue components of the color to be independently varied, with the effect shown on the screen.

Several predefined color constants can also be accessed via the colors resource in the API. For example, the name colors → blue refers to the color blue which has the ARGB encoding #FF0000FF. A complete list of the predefined colors which can be accessed via the colors resource is given in Appendix B.

Selecting Picture as the type for the *art* resource causes a menu of choices to be displayed. One choice, labeled upload, allows you to select an image on your device and upload it to a Microsoft website where it is accessible via its URL. Other choices allow images already available on the web to be selected. The image is then added to the Art section of the current script.

Selecting Sound as the type leads to similar choices as for an image.

Named constants of type Number and String are equally as accessible in a script as global data variables with these types. However data variables require initialization when the script is run, and they are not protected against being modified. A named constant, on the other hand, is initialized when the script is created and cannot be modified by assignments performed in the script.

The invalid value

The resource named invalid provides an invalid value specific to each datatype. For example, the following statement assigns the invalid value of type DateTime to variable x.

    x := invalid → datetime

A complete list of the possible invalid values provided by the invalid resource appears in Appendix B.

2.3.2   Variables

A script can access and assign to local variables, global data variables and parameters of the current action.

Local variables

Local variables follow the usual visibility rules and lifetime rules for block structured languages. The name of the variable is visible from the point of declaration down to the end of the block in which the declaration appears. Storage for the variable's value, if the type is a value type, is provided only while the block is active. If the type is a reference type, then storage for the reference is only provided while the block is active.

A local variable must be declared and initialized before it can be used. A declaration statement serves both purposes. For example, the following statement declares and initializes a String variable.

```
var s1 := "Hello!"
```

Following that declaration and down to the end of the enclosing block, the name s1 can be used to reference the local variable's current value.

Unlike most programming languages, the name s1 *cannot be hidden* by a declaration for another variable named s1 inside a nested block. The TouchDevelop editor simply does not permit two variables with the same name to be declared inside an action; it forces all the parameters and local variables in an action to have distinct names.

Global data variables

The **data** section of a script contains declarations for variables which are accessible by all actions within the script. Storage for these variables is permanently allocated in most cases, and would therefore persist between invocations of the script. However, variables which require significant storage and which are normally recomputed whenever the script is executed, such as an instance of the Board type, do not persist between uses of the script.

A global data variable is created either by tapping the *plus* button underneath the heading for the **data** section of the script or by declaring a local variable in an action or event and then using the 'promote to global' feature of the TouchDevelop editor.

A global data variable may be created with any datatype. If the type is Number, Boolean, String or DateTime, the variable has a neutral initial value. The value is 0, false, "" or 1 January 0001 12:00 am respectively. For any other datatype, the initial value is invalid.

An access to a global data variable inside a script is indicated by the special symbol ⌗. For example, the following statement assigns a value to a global variable of type Board.

```
⌗game := media → create board(480)
```

A reference to a global data variable is inserted into the script by tapping the keypad tile labeled ⌗data and then a tile labeled with the variable's name.

Action parameters
Parameters of an action are variables but with special properties. Zero or more input parameters and zero or more result parameters can be associated with the action by editing its properties. An input parameter can be added to an action by first displaying the code for the action, then tapping the first line of the action (where its name appears) to display information about the action. A plus button labeled "add input parameter" is displayed beneath that information. An input parameter can have any datatype except the Nothing type. A result parameter is similarly created by tapping the plus button labeled "add output parameter". It too can have any type other than Nothing.

A result parameter is special in that it has an initial value of invalid and that every execution path through the action must assign a value to it.

Other than that special requirement, the input parameters and the output parameters can be used within the action as though they were local variables.

2.3.3   Operators
With the exception of string concatenation, there are no implicit conversions; and none of the operators is overloaded. Therefore, except for string concatenation, each operator can be applied only to particular

datatypes. The operators and the associated datatypes for the operands and result are summarized in Table 2-6.

Table 2-6: Operators

Operator	Operand Types	Result Type	Description
+	Number	Number	prefix unary plus
-	Number	Number	prefix unary minus
+	Number Number	Number	addition
-	Number Number	Number	subtraction
*	Number Number	Number	multiplication
/	Number Number	Number	division
<	Number Number	Boolean	less-than comparison
≤	Number Number	Boolean	less-than-or-equal comparison
>	Number Number	Boolean	greater-than comparison
≥	Number Number	Boolean	greater-than-or-equal comparison
=	Number Number	Boolean	equals comparison
≠	Number Number	Boolean	not equals comparison
not	Boolean	Boolean	logical negation
and	Boolean Boolean	Boolean	logical and
or	Boolean Boolean	Boolean	logical or
‖	any any	String	string concatenation

The operands of the string concatenation operand may have *almost* any datatype. The values of the two operands are converted to type String before concatenation proceeds.

2.3.4   Calling an action
An action which has a single result parameter can be used in any context where an expression is permitted. Actions are covered in detail in section 2.5, below.

2.3.5   Calling an API method
The API provides many methods which return single results. An invocation of any of these methods can be used in a context where an expression is permitted. The methods may be associated with resources, such as media or languages, or they may be methods of datatypes defined in the API such as

Contact or Link Collection.

2.4   Statements

2.4.1   *Expression*

Any expression may be used as a statement. For example, this is a valid statement:

    "Hello " || " there!"

However, this particular statement is useless. The value of the expression is simply discarded. The use of an expression as a statement is only useful if evaluation of the statement has a side-effect. For example,

    ("Hello " || " there!") → post to wall

This expression evaluates to the special value nothing. However evaluation also has the side-effect of displaying a string on the screen.

An invocation of any action or API method which returns results can be used as a statement; the results are simply discarded.

2.4.2   *Declaration and assignment*

A declaration of a local variable is combined with an assignment to initialize the variable. The datatype of the initialization expression determines the datatype of the variable. For example, the following statement creates a local variable whose type is Location Collection.

    var places := collections → create location collection

Assignments may also assign values to existing variables. For example, the script can replace the value of the places variable declared above. A possible statement which does that is the following.

    places := invalid → location collection

If an action has more than one return parameter, an assignment statement can be used to assign all the results simultaneously. For example, if the script contains an action named Get Address Info which returns a String and a

Number as its two results, the action can be invoked with code like the following.

```
var street name := ""
var street number := 0
street name, street number := ▷Get Address Info("Joanie")
```

Either all the results or none of the results must be assigned. It is not possible to assign some results and discard the other results.

2.4.3   If statement

The TouchDevelop editor always generates the if-then-else form for an **if** statement, supplying empty bodies for the then clause and the else clause. Either or both of these clauses may subsequently be replaced with statement lists. The expression following the keyword if is an expression which must evaluate to a Boolean value. As usual, if the expression evaluates to true, the then clause is executed next and the else clause is skipped. Otherwise the reverse happens, the then clause is skipped and the else clause is executed.

For example, the following code determines the minimum of three values a, b and c.

```
if a < b then
    if a < c then
      min := a
    else
      min := c
else
    if b < c then
      min := b
    else
      min := c
```

2.4.4   While loop

A **while** loop has a controlling expression which must evaluate to a Boolean value. The loop body is repeatedly executed as long as the controlling expression evaluates to true.

For example, the following code searches for any song stored on a Windows phone whose duration exceeds 10 minutes.

```
var long song := invalid → song
var my music := media → songs
var num songs := my music → count
var i := 0
while i < num songs and long song → is invalid do
    var sng := my music → at(i)
    if sng→ duration > 10*60 then
      long song := sng
    else
      // do nothing
    i := i + 1
```

2.4.5   For loop

The **for** loop in TouchDevelop is similar to **for** loops in other programming languages, but with some added constraints. The index variable must be a Number; it must be initialized to zero for the first iteration and it must be incremented in steps of one.

An example **for** loop which sums the integers from 0 to 99 would be as follows.

```
var sum := 0
for 0 ≤ i < 100 do
    sum := sum + i
```

The index variable, i, in the example is a new local variable whose visibility is restricted to the **for** loop. It must be a uniquely named variable in the enclosing action. No assignments to the index variable are permitted within the loop body; this variable is restricted to being *read-only*.

2.4.6   For each loop

A **for each** loop is used for iterating through all the elements of a collection. For example, this loop adds up the playing times of all songs stored on a Windows phone.

```
var total := 0
for each sng in media→songs where true do
    total := total + sng → duration
    ("Total playing time = " || total/60 || " minutes") → post to wall
```

Note that there is a **where** clause which may be used to select only some of the values in the collection. The TouchDevelop editor supplies a default value of true for the **where** clause, but it can be replaced by any expression which evaluates to a Boolean value.

As with a **for** loop, the index variable is a read-only variable and it is a new local variable whose visibility is restricted to the for each loop.

2.5   Actions

2.5.1   *Defining an action*

An action can have zero or more input parameters and zero or more result parameters. When there are zero result parameters, the action can be called only for its side effects. There is no value returned by the call in this case. When the action has two or more result parameters, the invocation can be used on the right-hand side of a multiple assignment statement or the invocation can be made for its side effects only (and any returned results are ignored). When the action has exactly one result parameter, an invocation returns a single value as the result and that value may be used in any context where an expression can occur.

For example, consider the action Replicate defined as follows.

```
action Replicate( s: String, n: Number ) returns r: String
    r := ""
    while n > 0 do
        r := r || s
        n := n − 1
```

The action can be invoked and its resulting value used in a statement like the following.

```
("The answer is " || ▷Replicate("NO! ", 10) || "forever!")
    → post to wall
```

Immediately before the statements of the Replicate action are executed, the string "NO!" is copied into parameter s, 10 is copied into parameter n and the result parameter r is initialized to invalid. When the action has finished its execution, the final value of r is returned as the result.

Public versus private

When the properties of an action are accessed with the editor, the editor provides the ability to specify the input parameters, the result parameters, and to change the name of the action. There is also a checkbox which is labeled "*private action*". Leaving that box unchecked allows the action to be invoked directly. If a script has two or more actions (or *pages*, as discussed in Chapter 10) not tagged as private, the script has multiple entry points.

Another consequence of leaving the checkbox unticked is that the action can be invoked from another script when the script is published as a library. (See the subsection below on Library Scripts.)

Ticking the 'private action' checkbox restricts the action to being accessible only from other actions within the same script.

2.5.2   Call and return

An invocation of an action causes any arguments to be evaluated and copied to corresponding input parameters of the action, then the statements of the action are executed, and finally the values of any result parameters are copied back to the caller and made available as the value of the action.

A call to an action located in the same script is indicated by the code symbol, ▷.

2.5.3   Input parameters

The call by value parameter passing mechanism is used for input parameters. Each argument expression supplied by the caller is evaluated and assigned as an initial value to the corresponding parameter. In the case where the argument and parameter have a value type, a duplicate of the value is assigned to the parameter. When the argument and parameter have a reference type, it is the reference which is duplicated, so that the parameter references the same instance on the heap as supplied by the caller.

2.5.4   Result parameters

When an action is invoked, each result parameter is initialized to an invalid value of the correct type. There must be at least one assignment to each result parameter on every execution path which can be taken through the action. When control reaches the end of the action, the final values of the result parameters are returned as the results of the call.

2.5.5   Calling a library action

It is possible to invoke actions in a script which has been declared as a library. Each such library script must be added to the library section of the script. An imported script is given a name by the TouchDevelop editor (a name which is copied from the original script but can be changed later).

When editing code in the script, the editor provides a button labeled △libs. Tapping this key inserts the symbol △ into the code and the editor then provides a choice between the various names used for the imported library scripts. Once a name has been selected, the editor allows any action in that library script, other than those marked as private, to be called.

For example, the library script turtle, published as /sicm on the TouchDevelop website, provides actions for drawing colored lines using a virtual pen (a scheme known as 'turtle graphics'). To use this library in our own script S, one first adds the turtle script to the library section of S. The editor will use the name turtle for that library. Subsequently, actions and events defined in S can contain code like the following.

```
△turtle→initialize
△turtle→pen down
△turtle→pen color(colors→red)
△turtle→forward(100)
```

Rebinding libraries

If script S uses some actions in library L1 but another library L2 which implements the same actions becomes available, the editor provides the possibility to rebind S to use L2 instead of L1. A more complicated example of rebinding is possible if our script S uses library L1 and L1 in turns uses library L2. The libraries section of S can be edited so that references from L1 to actions in L2 can be bound instead to actions in another library L3 or to actions (with the correct signature) in S itself.

Visibility

Although the non-private actions of a library script are all visible, nothing else is visible. There is no direct access to any global data items or art items declared in the script. If the developer of the library wishes to permit such access, *get* and *set* actions must be provided in the library for returning or replacing the values of these items.

2.6   Events

In some respects, events are like actions. They contain code and some kinds of events take input parameters. However events cannot be called. They can only be invoked when something external to the script occurs. For example, shaking the phone is detected by the phone's sensors and can cause the code for the shake event in the TouchDevelop script to be executed.

An event interrupts the normal execution of a script. However an event will never interrupt the code for another event. Instead, execution of the second event will wait until the executing event has finished.

If a script contains code for one or more events, the script will not terminate execution when it reaches the end of the action which was initially invoked. The script enters an internal wait loop where it waits for events to occur and to be executed. To force a script to stop execution, it is necessary to use one of the API methods time→stop, time→stop and close or time→fail if not.

The kinds of events and brief descriptions are listed in Table 2-7. There are additional events, described in Table 2-8 which become available, if global data items of type Board and type Sprite Set have been declared. They are intended for use in games programs, and capture user interactions with the gameboard.

Table 2-7: Events

Event	Description of when invoked
gameloop	Invoked every 50 milliseconds. Intended for updating a game display, but usable for other purposes.
shake	Device is shaken
phone face up	Device is turned to be flat and face up
phone face down	Device is turned to be flat and face down
phone portrait	Device is turned upright
phone landscape left	Device is placed on its left side

phone landscape right	Device is placed on its right side
empty space on wall	The user has scrolled to the bottom of the wall and/or space to display new output has become available
page navigated from	The page displayed on the screen has been popped
active song changed	The song being played by the phone has changed
player state changed	The media player starts playing
camera button pressed	Camera button on phone is pressed
camera button half pressed	Camera button on phone is halfway pressed
camera button released	Camera button on phone is released
tap wall *XXX* (item: *XXX*)	A value of type *XXX* displayed on the wall is tapped; this value is received as the input parameter. There is a different tap wall event for various types, represented by XXX.

The tap wall XXX event in Table 2-7 represents many events, where XXX can be any of the types Appointment, Camera, Color, Contact, Device, Link, Media Player, Message, Page Button, Picture, Picture Album, Place, Playlist, Printer, Song, Sound, String, TextBox, Tile, Vector3 or any object type defined in the Records section of the script.

Table 2-8: Gameboard events

Event	Description
tap board(x: Number, y: Number)	The gameboard has been tapped at coordinates x, y.
swipe board(x: Number, y: Number, delta x: Number, delta y: Number)	The gameboard has been swiped, starting at coordinates x, y and continuing along the vector delta x, delta y.
tap sprite in sprite set(sprite: Sprite, index in set: Number, x: Number, y: Number)	A sprite in the sprite set has been tapped; the first two parameters specify which sprite and the last two give the x, y coordinates of the sprite.

Event	Description
swipe sprite in sprite set(sprite: Sprite, index in set: Number, x: Number, y: Number, delta x: Number, delta y: Number)	A sprite in the sprite set has been swiped; the first two parameters specify which sprite, the next two give the x, y coordinates of the sprite, and the last two give the vector describing the swipe motion.
drag sprite in sprite set(sprite: Sprite, index in set: Number, x: Number, y: Number, delta x: Number, delta y: Number)	A sprite in the sprite set has been dragged; the first two parameters specify which sprite, the next two give the x, y coordinates of the sprite, and the last two give the vector describing the dragging motion.

2.7   Pages

Pages are a recent addition to the TouchDevelop language. They provide the script writer with the tools to develop sophisticated user interfaces. Pages are added to a script in a similar way to actions or events and, like them, contain statements to be executed.

A syntactic construct **boxed** is used as a wrapper for statement lists inside a page, where those statements create the content and style of a rectangular region of the screen display.

Pages and the **boxed** construct are covered in detail in Chapter 10.

2.8   Creating library scripts

When a script's properties are edited, there is an opportunity to tick a box labeled 'this script is a library'. This enables all actions not flagged as private to be callable from other scripts on your phone. Publishing the script on the TouchDevelop website will allow other users to access the public actions included in the script.

Implementation restrictions on libraries

A library script cannot define any entries in its Events or Records sections. Items in the Data or Art sections of the library script can be directly accessed from other scripts. If such access is desirable, then additional actions to provide the desired form of access must be defined.

Chapter 3
The Wall – using the screen

A TouchDevelop script usually needs to interact with the user. While input via a microphone and output via speakers built into, or connected to, the device are certainly possibilities, a touchscreen or a screen plus a mouse is almost always used for input and output. In TouchDevelop, the screen is known as the wall. The API provides many ways in which a script can access the wall.

3.1   Output – the writing on the wall

3.1.1   Output of simple values

Every datatype in TouchDevelop provides a method named post to wall. If that method is called, some representation of the value is displayed. Here are some simple examples.

```
action main()
    (1/3) → post to wall
    123 → post to wall
    ("hello" || " there") → post to wall
```

(11>11) → post to wall

The code produces a result like that shown in Figure 3-1 on the left side. Note that the output is apparently displayed in reverse order. That is because the default is for each new output item to be inserted at the top of the screen, pushing previously generated output further down. The default is a good one if it is desired that the user can see the most recent item without having to scroll down.

Figure 3-1: Simple output, normal and reversed order

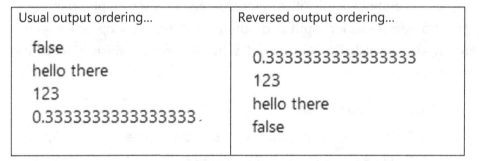

Usual output ordering...	Reversed output ordering...
false hello there 123 0.3333333333333333 .	0.3333333333333333 123 hello there false

To display a value in a manner which stands out prominently on the screen, a TextBox value can be used. The text can be displayed in any color, with any size font, against any background color. A simple example of using a TextBox to display a string is shown in Figure 3-2. The script is shown on the left and the result of running it is shown on the right.

Figure 3-2: Displaying a string using a TextBox

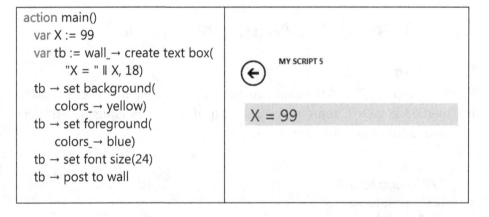

```
action main()
    var X := 99
    var tb := wall_→ create text box(
        "X = " ‖ X, 18)
    tb → set background(
        colors_→ yellow)
    tb → set foreground(
        colors_→ blue)
    tb → set font size(24)
    tb → post to wall
```

MY SCRIPT 5

X = 99

3.1.2   Direction of Output

The default direction of output on the screen can be changed so that items are displayed from top-to-bottom. To do so, make the method call:

```
wall →set reversed(true)
```

The following sample script should make the effect clear.

```
action main()
    (1/3)→post to wall
    123→post to wall
    wall →set reversed(true)
    ("hello" || " there") →post to wall
    (11>11) →post to wall
```

The result of running the script is shown in Figure 3-1 on the right side. Comparison of the two snapshots shows that the call affected all output on the screen – not just the output generated after the call was made.

In summary, the effect of making the call with an argument of true is to cause existing output on the screen to be reordered if necessary, so that the oldest output is at the top and the newest output is at the bottom. Future calls to

```
post to wall
```

cause the new output to be added at the bottom. Making the call

```
wall →set reversed(false)
```

reorders the output again so that the oldest output is at the bottom and the newest is at the top, then subsequent calls to post to wall will again cause output to be inserted at the top of the screen.

3.1.3   Output of composite values

Displaying a composite value such as one with the DateTime or Vector3 type produces an appropriately formatted result. Displaying a collection of values produces a list of items on the screen, each element formatted in the appropriate manner for the element's datatype.

Figure 3-3 gives a few examples of composite values being displayed.

Figure 3-3: Displaying composite values

action main()
    var v := collections →
        create number collection
    v → add(123)
    v → add(456)
    v → add(- 789)
    v → post to wall
    var dt := time → today
    dt → post to wall
    var m := math →
        create matrix(2,3)
    m → set item(0, 2, 3.142)
    m → set item(1, 0, 2.718)
    m → post to wall
	[0, 0, 3.142
	2.718, 0, 0]
	Tue May 21 2013 00:00:00 GMT-0700 (Pacific Daylight Time)
	[123, 456, -789]

3.1.4   Output of media values

Each media value is displayed on the screen in a manner appropriate for the datatype. In the case of a Song or a Song Album value, there is also a play button displayed. Tapping that play button causes the song or the song album to be played.

A summary of what is displayed for each datatype is given in Table 3-1.

Table 3-1: Display of media values

Datatype	What is displayed
Picture	The picture, resized if necessary to fit the screen.
Board	The board (note that the board can be changed and redisplayed dynamically).
Song	A play button plus whichever of these items is available: duration, artist, name of album from which the song was obtained, the album cover, track number.
Sound	The text "A sound..." and a button to play the sound.
Picture Album	A sequence of all pictures in the album.
Song Album	A play button plus whichever of these items if available: total duration, artist, name of album, the album cover, number of tracks.

3.1.5   Output of social values

Each value managed by the social API is displayed in a manner appropriate for the datatype. The Contact and Link values include buttons which can be tapped to initiate a phone call or send a message.

A summary of what is displayed for each datatype is given in Table 3-2.

Table 3-2: Display of social values

Datatype	What is displayed
Appointment	The date, time and details of the appointment.
Contact	The name of the contact plus buttons which can be tapped to initiate a phone call or send a SMS message or send an email to this contact .
Link	The name associated with the link plus a button to initiate a phone call, send a SMS message or send an email, depending on the kind of link.
Location	A scrollable Bing map which shows the location.
Message	The name of the sender, the time when the message was sent plus the contents of the message.
Place	The name associated with the place plus a thumbnail map showing the location of the place.

3.1.6   Output of web values

There are several datatypes specifically associated with web access. Values of five of these types are displayed on the wall according to Table 3-3.

Table 3-3: Display of web values

Datatype	What is displayed
Form Builder	The current contents of the form
Json Object	The string value of the JSON object.
Web Request	Two lines which display the accepted webpage encodings followed by a line which contains the keyword GET followed by a URL.
Web Response	The response
Xml Object	The string value of the XML object

3.2   Input of values from the touchscreen

The wall API provides several methods which prompt the user to enter a value or pick a value from a range of possibilities. These methods are listed in Table 3-4. Some sample statements to illustrate their use are shown in Figure 3-4.

Table 3-4: Prompting for input

Datatype	Method	Description
Boolean	ask boolean	An OK button and a Cancel button are displayed. Tapping OK returns true and tapping Cancel returns false
Number	ask number	The user is prompted to enter a number, which is returned as the result
String	ask string	The user is prompted to enter a string which is returned as the result
DateTime	pick date	The user is prompted to pick a date; that date combined with a time of 12 noon is returned as the result
String	pick string	A list of strings is displayed and the user is prompted to pick one; the index of the selected string is returned as the result
DateTime	pick time	The user is prompted to pick a time of day; that time combined is with an undefined date and returned as the result

3.3   Updating the wall's content

Each call of post to wall adds a new item on the screen. However it is frequently the case that we wish to leave the number of items unchanged and simply alter the value of one of them. The simplest, least sophisticated and least efficient way to achieve that effect would be to invoke

wall → clear

and then re-display all the items with their new values.

However, TouchDevelop provides some alternatives which should be preferred.

Figure 3-4: Prompting for input

```
action main( )
    wall → set reversed(true)
    "Name three friends ..." → post to wall
    var names := collections → create string collection
    for 0 ≤ i < 3 do
        names → add( wall → ask string( "Enter next name: " ) )
    var x := wall → pick string( "Choose one of these people",
        "Names", names )
    var who := names → at(x)
    var dt := wall → pick date("What is " || who || "\'s birthday?",
        "Year / Month / Date")
    // Note: this outputs a date as Day/Month/Year
    (who || "\'s birthday is " || dt → day || "/" || dt → month ||
        "/" || dt → year) → post to wall
```

3.3.1   *Updatable textbox*

For the display of text which needs to be changed while the script is executing, a textbox provides an easy-to-use mechanism. Figure 3-5 shows a simple script which displays a line of text on the screen and then changes the text when the page button at the bottom is tapped.

The call to the set text method of the textbox causes the string displayed on the screen to be updated immediately. It is also possible to change the size of the text and the colors used in the textbox on the fly. Note that if the same textbox value has been posted to the wall more than once, then the set text method will cause all of those occurrences on the wall to be updated.

Figure 3-5: An updatable textbox (/censaair)

```
action main( )
    ▣ tb := wall → create text box("Tap the plus button below", 20)
    ▣ tb → set border(colors → blue)
    ▣ tb → post to wall
```

```
wall → add button("add", "Tap Here")

event tap wall Page Button ( item : Page Button )
    ⊞ tb → set text("I have been tapped!")
    ⊞ tb → set foreground(colors → red)

data tb : TextBox
```

3.3.2   Updating a board display

For updating more sophisticated displays of information on the screen, an instance of the Board datatype is normally used. Pictures, text messages and shapes can all be drawn on the board as sprites. Each sprite can have its position, orientation or content changed individually. Then a call to the update on wall method of the board causes a rendering of the board on the screen to be immediately updated. Although the main usage of the Board datatype was intended to be for implementing games, it is useful in any situation where information displayed on the screen needs to be changed.

A re-implementation of the previous example where a board is used instead is shown in Figure 3-6. The use of a board and sprites provides much greater flexibility because the positions and orientations of the items on the screen can also be updated.

Figure 3-6: Updating text using a board (/wkoxnasz)

```
action main( )
    ▣ board := media → create board(200)
    ▣ sprite := ▣ board → create text(200, 20, 30, "Tap the plus button")
    ▣ sprite → set pos(100, 10)
    ▣ sprite → set color(colors → blue)
    ▣ board → post to wall
    wall → add button("add", "Tap Here")

event tap wall Page Button( item : Page Button )
    ▣ sprite → set text("I have been tapped")
    ▣ sprite → set color(colors → red)
    ▣ board → update on wall

data board : Board
data sprite : Sprite
```

3.4   Events on the touchscreen

3.4.1   Tap wall events

A script can receive input via tap events on the screen. There is one event type for nearly every kind of value which can be displayed on the screen. A full list is provided in Table 3-5.

If one of these values is displayed on the screen, then tapping the value will cause the corresponding event to be executed. The tapped item is passed as a parameter to the event. The normal parameter passing rules are used, implying that a copy of the value is passed if the item is a value type and a reference to the value is passed if the item is a reference type. A trivial script which shows the use of tap events to select a string is shown in Figure 3-7.

Figure 3-7: Using tap wall events

```
action main( )
    "One" → post to wall
    "Two" → post to wall
    "Three" → post to wall

event tap wall String( item: String )
    ("\"" ‖ item ‖ "\" was tapped") → post to wall
```

3.4.2   Tap board events

Although it is easy to display values on the screen and associate 'tap wall' events with them, there is very little control over where the values are positioned. To achieve full control over placement, it is necessary to display the values as sprites on an instance of the Board datatype. If the script displays the board with its sprites on the screen, then tapping or swiping or dragging one of the sprites will trigger an event that can be captured by the script.

A trivial script which brightens or darkens the color of a solid rectangle when buttons are tapped is shown in Figure 3-8.

Table 3-5: Tap wall events

Event	What happens
tap wall Appointment	
tap wall Camera	
tap wall Color	
tap wall Contact	Each event receives a single parameter. That
tap wall Link	parameter has the datatype named in the event.
tap wall Message	When any value of this type is tapped on the
tap wall Motion	screen, the corresponding event is triggered. For
tap wall Page Button	value types, a copy of the value which was tapped
tap wall Picture	is passed as the parameter. For reference types, a
tap wall Picture Album	reference to the tapped value is passed as the
tap wall Place	parameter.
tap wall Playlist	
tap wall Song	
tap wall Song Album	

Event	What happens
tap wall Sound	
tap wall String	
tap wall TextBox	
tap wall Vector3	

Simply defining a variable with a datatype of Board or Sprite or Sprite Set in the data section of the script causes new event types to be made available. In the case of the script shown in Figure 3-7, the data section contains three sprites named rectangle, Lighter and Darker, it contains controls which has type Sprite Set, and board which has type Board.

The existence of these globally visible data variables creates 14 events with these names:

- tap sprite: rectangle, swipe sprite: rectangle, drag sprite: rectangle
- tap sprite: Lighter, swipe sprite: Lighter, drag sprite: Lighter
- tap sprite: Darker, swipe sprite: Darker, drag sprite: Darker
- tap sprite in controls, swipe sprite in controls, drag sprite in controls
- tap board: board, swipe board: board

Figure 3-8: Using sprite events (/akmcnpux)

```
action main( )
    ▣board := media → create board(640)
    ▣rectangle := ▣board → create rectangle(300, 200)
    ▣rectangle → set color(colors → from rgb(0.5, 0.5, 0.5))
    ▣rectangle → set pos(200, 200)
    ▣lighter := ▣board → create text(100, 20, 40, "Lighter")
    ▣darker := ▣board → create text(100, 20, 40, "Darker")
    ▣lighter → set color(colors → foreground)
    ▣darker → set color(colors → foreground)
    ▣lighter → set pos(100, 400)
    ▣darker → set pos(300, 400)
    ▣controls := ▣board → create sprite set
    ▣controls → add(▣lighter)
    ▣controls → add(▣darker)
    ▣board → post to wall

event tap sprite in controls(
    sprite: Sprite , index in set: Number,  x: Number,  y: Number )
    var delta := 0.2
    if index in set = 0 then
        ▣rectangle → set color(▣rectangle → color → lighten(delta))
    else
        ▣rectangle → set color(▣rectangle → color → darken(delta))
    ▣board → update on wall
```

For sprites, the event names have the pattern tap/swipe/drag sprite: xxx where xxx is the name of the sprite. For sprite sets, the names have the pattern tap/swipe/drag sprite in YYY where YYY is the name of the set. For boards, the names have the pattern tap/swipe board: ZZZ where ZZZ is the name of the board. Parameters passed to each event identify which sprite was touched (when it is a sprite set event), the coordinates of the sprite on the board, and the extent of a swiping or a dragging action.

Note that there are yet more events associated with the Board datatype which have not been listed here, including the possibility of tapping anywhere on the board (not just on a sprite) and obtaining the coordinates of where the screen was tapped.

3.5   Pushing and popping pages

Some scripts may need to display information temporarily and then have it disappear. Or, perhaps, there is a need to input some extra information from the user but it is undesirable to disrupt what has already been displayed on the screen. The solution, for situations like these, is to create a brand new wall on which information is displayed and input is requested, then have that wall disappear and have the original wall re-displayed.

The general facility takes the form of a stack of pages. Each page corresponds to an instance of the wall.

The following command creates a new empty wall.

    wall → push new page

The script can then proceed to display information or prompt for input on this new wall. Afterwards, the following command

    wall → pop page

will delete that new wall and revert to displaying the previous version.

Some additional methods associated with the wall API are wall→pages which returns the stack of pages as a collection, and wall→current page which gets the current page.

3.6   Titles and subtitles

The output from a script can be beautified by displaying a title at the top of the screen. If appropriate, a subtitle may be displayed too. A few lines of code which illustrate the features are as follows.

```
wall → set title("The wall's title")
wall → set subtitle("The subtitle")
"First line of output" → post to wall
"Second line of output" → post to wall
```

The result of running this code appears in Figure 3-9. Note that the capitalization of the title and subtitle has been changed; they have both been converted to lowercase.

Figure 3-9: Title and subtitle example

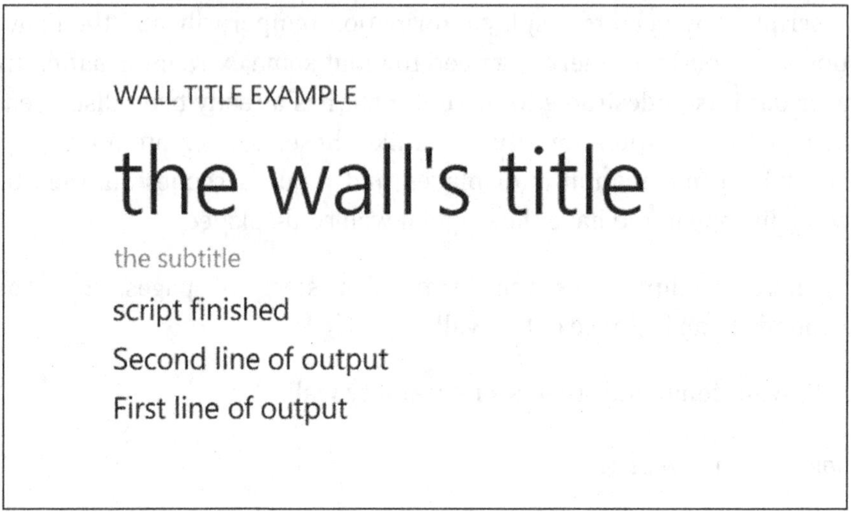

WALL TITLE EXAMPLE

the wall's title

the subtitle

script finished

Second line of output

First line of output

3.7   Wall buttons

Buttons in the form of simple icons may be displayed at the bottom of the screen. These are *page buttons*. Tapping a button triggers an event which can be captured in the script. The icons are predefined and have names. The names are as follows.

"add", "back", "cancel", "check", "close", "delete", "download",
"edit", "favs.addto", "favs", "feature.camera", "feature.email",
"feature.search", "feature.settings", "feature.video", "folder",
"minus", "new", "next", "questionmark", "refresh", "save",
"share", "stop", "sync", "transport.ff", "transport.pause",
"transport.play", "transport.rew", "upload"

This list of names can be generated by executing the following statement.

    wall → button icon names → post to wall

A possible statement to generate a button is the following.

    wall → add button("questionmark", "help?")

Executing that statement causes the bar at the bottom of the screen to contain a 'question mark' icon with the label "help?" as shown in Figure 3-

10.

Figure 3-10: The 'Question Mark' page button

There is space for several page buttons at the bottom of the screen. Therefore the event triggered when a page button is tapped has a parameter which enables the button to be identified, that parameter being the string used as the label. The following code shows how an event can distinguish between different possibilities for the button.

```
event tap wall Page Button(item: Page Button)
    if (item → icon → equals("help?") then
        ▷show help info
    else
        if (item → icon → equals("cancel") then
            time → stop
        else
            // do nothing
```

The methods provided for the Page Button datatype are listed in Table 3-6.

Table 3-6: Methods of the Page Table datatype

Page Table Method	Description
equals(page button : Page Button) : Boolean	Returns true if this button is the same button as the one passed as a parameter
icon : String	Gets the name of the icon
page : Page	Gets the page to which this button is attached
text : String	Gets the text associated with the icon

3.8   On-demand creation of output

Some scripts may need to generate a lot of output which the user will need to scroll through. It may be a waste of processing time (and perhaps battery charge) if all that output is generated at once. A better approach would be to create chunks of output only as the user scrolls to view the part of the screen where the output would be displayed.

An event empty space on wall is triggered whenever there is space on the wall for displaying new output. There will be space when the user scrolls to the end of the displayed output.

Chapter 4
The Web

Most mobile devices can be connected to the internet, either via a Wi-Fi connection or by using the data services of the cellphone company. Many useful scripts already exist to retrieve information from websites on the internet. By using the facilities of TouchDevelop, you can easily construct the additional scripts which extract the specific information you might need. Another common use of an internet connection is to share information via one's Twitter or Facebook account. TouchDevelop provides facilities for uploading messages to your account.

4.1   URLs and webpages

4.1.1   Working with URLs
The TouchDevelop API provides an easy way to interact with software installed on your device to access the web. Most of these interactions begin with a URL. Here is an example of one of the simplest things we can do in a script – opening the web browser at a particular webpage.

```
If not web→is connected then
        "Sorry, you don't have an internet connection!" → post to wall
        time → stop
else
        // do nothing
```

web → browse("http://touchdevelop.com")

Most web interactions in a TouchDevelop script need a URL to specify a web address. Two API methods which assist in working with URLs are listed in Table 4-1. Frequently, it is necessary to include some special characters in a URL.

Table 4-1: Converting URLs

Method	Description
web→url encode(s : String) : String	Encode special characters so that they can be included in a URL.
Web→url decode(url : String) : String	Decodes a URL back to a normal string containing special characters.

4.1.2   Creating and using web-based links

One use of the Link datatype in TouchDevelop is to save links to people in the form of their email addresses or their phone numbers. This usage is covered in Chapter 8. Another use is to save links to materials found on the web, such as videos, pictures, and webpages in general. The web resource in the TouchDevelop API provides methods for creating links in the latter category. Some more methods will search for webpages or web resources and return a collection of links to the results. These methods are listed in Table 4-2.

The Link datatype combines additional information with an address such as a URL. It can optionally have an associated name and a location (which is usually relevant for a photograph but is certainly not restricted to photographs). Methods are provided for setting and getting this additional information.

Note that no checking on the validity of the URL is performed when the Link instance is created. The URL is simply held as a string, and can be accessed as a string by using the address method.

Example: The script *flickr search* (/atue) provides an example of a library which creates a Link Collection instance containing references to particular kinds of images, and the script *flickr slideshow* (/fluo) uses that library to generate a slideshow of images on a theme provided by the user.

Table 4-2: Creating web links

Method	Description
web→link image(url : String) : Link	Create a link to a picture
web→link media(url : String) : Link	Create a link to an audio file or a video
web→link url(name : String, url : String) : Link	Create a link to a webpage and associate a name with this link
web→search(terms : String) : Link Collection	Use Bing to search for webpages matching the search terms
web→search images(terms : String) : Link Collection	Use Bing to search for images matching the search terms
web→search images nearby(terms : String, location : Location, distance : Number) : Link Collection	Use Bing to search for images matching the search terms and associated with a location within a given distance of a specified location
web→search nearby(terms : String, location : Location, distance : Number) : Link Collection	Use Bing to search for webpages matching the search terms and associated with a location within a given distance of a particular location
web→search news(terms : String) : Link Collection	Use Bing to search for news items matching the search terms
web→search news nearby(terms : String, location : Location, distance : Number) : Link Collection	Use Bing to search for news items matching the search terms and associated with a location within a given distance of a specified location

Using the wall with web-based links

The wall can be used to hold links to websites in general or to various kinds of resources that may be downloaded. For example, to display an image when an instance of the Link type has been provided, code like the following may be used.

```
// link (of type Link) refers to an image on a website
var pic := web → download picture(link → address)
wall → set background picture(pic)
```

Here are some more examples. The following script lines (extracted from the script /hrvg held on the TouchDevelop Samples website) demonstrate some interesting possibilities.

```
// 1. This creates a basic internet link which is opened in the browser
//   when the link is tapped
web → link url("This is a link to TouchDevelop", "http://touchdevelop.com") →
post to wall
```

```
// 2. This will load and display an image from the web
//   when the link is tapped
web → link image("http://www.touchdevelop.com/Images/title1.png") → post to
wall
```

```
// 3. You can also link to a movie or a sound file through the link
//   media method. It will be played when the link is tapped
web → link media(
"http://media.ch9.ms/ch9/06b9/1669dae1-2b5f-4858-abee-9ea7018806b9/
WP7Pex4FunPeliNikolai_ch9.wmv") → post to wall
```

If the first of the examples above is run as a script, the result displayed on the screen looks similar to Figure 4-1. Tapping the 'go' button on the right causes the webpage to be displayed.

Figure 4-1: Posting a Webpage Link to the wall

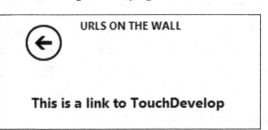

Running the second example displays the image which is downloaded from the web. The result of running it as a script looks similar to Figure 4-2. (The image looks fuzzy because the original is a small low resolution image which gets scaled up in size before being displayed the screen.)

Figure 4-2: Posting a link to an image on the wall

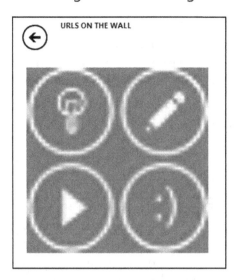

4.1.3   *Checking the internet connection*

Your device can usually access the internet via a Wi-Fi connection or through a cellphone connection. However there will be occasions when there is no internet connectivity. A script should test whether there is connectivity before proceeding to try to access web resources. The API method call

web → is connected

returns true or false to indicate the current situation.

The following API method call should provide information about the kind of connection, if one exists. The result will be one of the strings "unknown" "none" "ethernet" "wifi" or "mobile".

web → connection type

Finally, the script can discover the name of the Wi-Fi service or the cellphone service which is handling internet requests. The following API method call returns a string with the name of that service, if there is one. If no name can be found, the result is an empty string.

web → connection name

4.2   Downloading and uploading files

If a script accesses the internet, it is quite likely that information in some form needs to be downloaded. Sometimes information needs to be uploaded too. The TouchDevelop API provides several upload and download methods appropriate for accessing different kinds of web resources. These methods are summarized in Table 4-3 and then described in more detail in the following subsections.

Table 4-3: Uploading/downloading to websites

Method	Description
web → download(url : String) : String	Uses a HTTP GET request to obtain a HTML-encoded webpage as a string.
web → download json(url : String) : Json Object	Uses a HTTP GET request to read a JSON data structure
web → download picture(url : String) : Picture	Downloads a picture
web → download song(url : String, name : String) : Song	Creates a streamed song file; the download is delayed until the song is played
web → download sound(url : String) : Sound	Downloads a sound in WAV format
web → upload(url : String, body : String) : String	Uses a HTTP POST request to upload string data to a website service; the result is a response string from that service
web → upload picture(url : String, pic : Picture): String	Uses a HTTP POST request to upload a picture to a website service; the result is a response string

4.2.1   Downloading a text file or downloading HTML

The simplest format for a web resource is a text file. If the URL ends with the suffix ".txt" or ".text" then the web resource is almost certainly a plain ASCII (or UTF8) text file. However the URL does not necessarily need either of these suffixes to refer to a text file.

A webpage which contains HTML is also a text file; it is simply text which includes extra commands to specify the structure and the format of the webpage when displayed by a browser. If it is useful, the raw HTML can be read as though it were a text file.

A TouchDevelop script can download a text file or a HTML page and read it into a String variable using script lines similar to those shown in this example:

```
action main( )
  var s := web →
      download("http://www.smlnj.org/doc/FAQ/faq.txt")
  if s → is invalid then
    "unable to read webpage" → post to wall
  else
    // ... proceed to use the string s
    "" → post to wall
    s → substring(0,100) → post to wall
    "First 100 characters are:" → post to wall
    ("Length = " || s → count) → post to wall
```

When this script is run, the result looks as shown in Figure 4-3. Most likely, though, your script will proceed to do something more complicated with the string than just display the total length and the first 100 characters.

Figure 4-3: Downloading a text file

```
Length = 81201
First 100 characters are:
1. Language

1.1. Core

1.1.1. Types and type checking

Q: [value restriction]
Why do the following
```

4.2.2   Downloading a picture

A variety of formats are used for encoding pictures as computer files. The commonly used formats are JPEG, GIF, PNG, BMP, TIFF and WMP. They are all supported by TouchDevelop. If the filename or URL ends with the suffix

".jpg", ".jpeg", ".gif", ".png", ".bmp" or ".wmp" then one of these formats has been used, and the methods provided in the TouchDevelop API should be able to download and manipulate the picture.

The script statements are similar to before, but use a different method so that the result is obtained as a Picture value (and not as a String value).

```
action main( )
    var pic := web → download picture(
        "http://www.touchdevelop.com/Images/title2.png")
    if pic → is invalid then
        "Unable to download picture" → post to wall
    else
        // ... proceed to use the picture pic in some way
        pic → post to wall
        ("Image dimensions = " || pic → width || " x " || pic → height) →
            post to wall
```

Running this particular script yields the result shown in Figure 4-4.

Figure 4-4: Picture download

Image dimensions = 314 x 47

touchdevelop

4.2.3   *Downloading sounds and music*

TouchDevelop and the Windows phone software support two kinds of audio files – short sound clips and longer audio tracks which would usually contain music (or spoken voice). In TouchDevelop, these correspond to values with type Sound and type Song respectively.

If the filename or URL ends with the suffix ".wav" then the file contents are in the 'Waveform Audio File' (WAV) format and it is material that can be downloaded as a Sound value. A Sound value can *only* be created from a WAV file. If the suffix is ".mp3" then the material is in an audio format commonly used for music and the spoken word. This material can be downloaded as a Song value.

Some code to download and play a sound effect is shown below. (The sound effect used in this example comes from the website "Partners in Rhyme" which provides royalty-free music and sound-effects.)

```
action getSound( )
    var snd := web → download sound( "http://www.sound-effect.com/
pirsounds/WEB_DESIGN_SOUNDS_WAV1/SOUNDFX/TOYLASER.WAV" )
        if snd → is invalid then
            "unable to download sound" → post to wall
        else
        // ... proceed to use the sound value snd
        snd → set volume(0.7)
        snd → play
        ("Duration = " || snd → duration) → post to wall
```

Example: A script to access and play a song is available as *Stream mp3 from internet* (/ncwo). The script includes some extra features to make it a bit more useful. These are events to suspend the playback and to stop the playback permanently. When the script is run, the URL can be provided as an argument. If no URL is provided, the last used URL is used again.

4.2.4   *Uploading strings and files*

Two API methods are available for uploading material to a website. One method uploads a string and the other uploads a picture. Both use the HTPP POST protocol for the uploads. Typically, uploads will be performed when interacting with a website which follows the REST guidelines (as covered below).

Here are sample statements which use the API method call for uploading a string.

```
var info := "name=an+other&age=37&car=Ford+Mustang"
// upload key-value pairs in the info string to website  specified by the url
var response string := web → upload( url, info )
```

The website which receives the POST request will pass the string onto a program for processing and a string returned by the program comes back as the result of this API call.

Uploading a picture is similar. The sample script *web stuff* (/hrvg) is an example of uploading a picture of a QR code in the JPEG format to a website.

4.3   Downloading structured data

The internet makes a wealth of information available to your script. The difficult part is in extracting the information you need from a website. Suppose that you want your script to look up the current temperature in some location. There are many websites you could use to find this information, one of them is local.msn.com. For example, if you point your browser at the URL   http://local.msn.com/weather.aspx?q=redmond-wa&zip= 98052, it will display a webpage containing much information about current weather conditions in Redmond, but where only a tiny part of the page shows the temperature. A snapshot showing just a small part of this web page is reproduced in Figure 4-5.

We can, in principle, use the API call web→download to fetch the HTML code for the webpage as one very long string of characters. Then we can write some statements which search the HTML code for the little snippet of information that we need. In this example, we need to search the code for a sequence of characters with a structure like the following.

```
<span class="curtemp">53°F</span>
```

Here the two *characters* '53' are the data we want to extract and convert to the *number* 53. You have to study the HTML code for the website to figure out what sequence of characters would be sufficient to accomplish the task, and no two websites are going to be the same. The script may also need to untranslate characters which have been replaced by HTML escape sequences. For example, an ampersand character displayed on a webpage appears in the HTML code as the five characters "&". The API provides two methods for converting between special characters and their HTML escape sequences. These are web→html decode and web→html encode.

Figure 4-5: Snapshot of a weather webpage

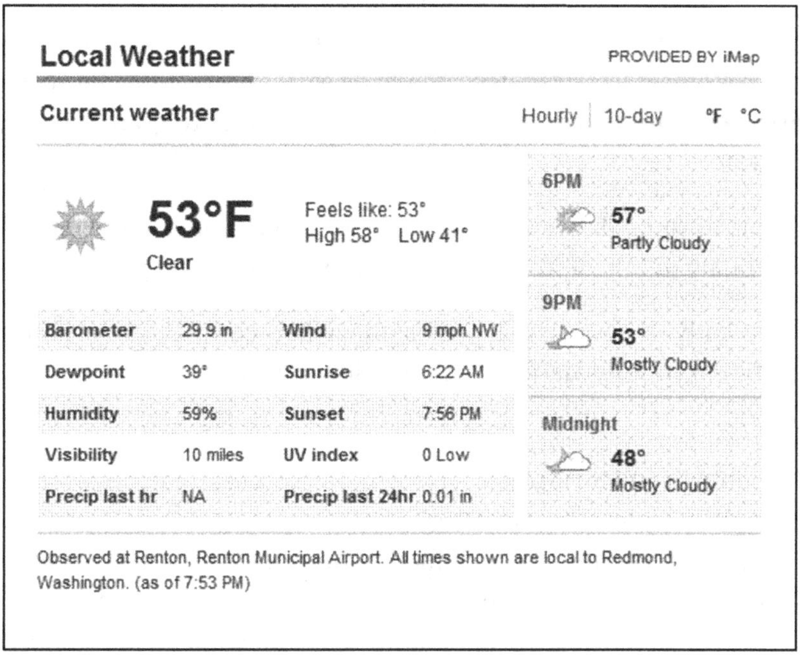

The kind of programming which analyzes webpages to extract information is known as *web scraping* (or *web harvesting*). You should write code like this only if there is no alternative and, even then, think twice. This is a job best left for professionals who have access to special software, and it is a job which has to be repeated whenever the web designers choose to change the layout of the website being accessed.

What can we do instead? The best answer is to find an internet site which serves up the information you need in a more easily digestible format. Two formats, widely used for delivering information in a systematic and simple manner, are XML and JSON.

Both these formats are supported by TouchDevelop, and will be explained with simple examples in the following sections of this chapter. In the particular case where we need to find the current weather in some location, there are several suitable websites. One of them is 'The Weather Channel' but, unfortunately access to this service requires a monthly subscription. A free alternative is Weather2 which supplies both JSON and XML: http://www.myweather2.com/developer/

4.3.1   *Downloading information in JSON format*

JSON is short for *JavaScript Object Notation*. It is a text format which borrows notations and data structuring ideas from the JavaScript scripting language. It is a format which has been designed to be easy for processing by computer software (and therefore by TouchDevelop scripts too), but is human-readable too.

An example of some data expressed in JSON format appears in Figure 4-6. It is weather data obtained from the weather2 service.

There are only a few simple rules for what constitutes a valid JSON representation of information. A file in JSON format contains the following elements.

- Numbers and Strings
- Boolean values (true or false)
- Arrays – written as a sequence of array elements separated by commas, with the whole sequence enclose in square brackets
- Objects – written as an unordered collection of key-value pairs where a colon separates each key from the value, each pair is separated from the next by a comma, and the whole collection is enclosed in curly braces; the keys must be written as strings and they must be distinct from each other.
- The special value *null*, meaning empty.

Referring back to Figure 4-6, we can see that the figure shows an object with just one key-value pair, where the key is "weather" and the associated value is another object. That object contains two key-value pairs; one key is "curren_weather" and the other is "forecast". The value associated with "curren_weather" is an array that contains just one element, which is an object. The value associated with "forecast" is an array containing two elements, and the two elements are objects with identical structures. (The elements do not need to have the same structure, or even have the same types, but processing the JSON file is easier if they do.)

- If we have found a website which provides results in JSON format, we can access it using the call web→download json. Here is an example invocation.

Figure 4-6: Weather data in JSON format

```
{ "weather":
  { "curren_weather": [
      { "humidity": "87", "pressure": "1005", "temp": "6",
        "temp_unit": "c", "weather_code": "1",
        "weather_text": "Partly cloudy",
        "wind": [ {"dir": "ENE", "speed": "4", "wind_unit": "kph" } ]
      } ],
    "forecast": [
      { "date": "2012-04-14",  "day": [
        { "weather_code": "2", "weather_text": "Cloudy skies",
          "wind": [ {"dir": "NNE", "dir_degree": "26", "speed": "14",
            "wind_unit": "kph" } ]
        } ],
        "day_max_temp": "12",  "night": [
          { "weather_code": "2", "weather_text": "Cloudy skies",
            "wind": [ {"dir": "NNE", "dir_degree": "18", "speed": "14",
            "wind_unit": "kph" } ]
          } ],
        "night_min_temp": "1", "temp_unit": "c"
      },
      { "date": "2012-04-15",  "day": [
        { "weather_code": "80", "weather_text": "Light rain shower",
          "wind": [ {"dir": "N", "dir_degree": "8", "speed": "25",
          "wind_unit": "kph" } ]
        } ],
        "day_max_temp": "9",  "night": [
          { "weather_code": "0", "weather_text": "Clear skies",
            "wind": [ {"dir": "NNW", "dir_degree": "359", "speed": "25",
            "wind_unit": "kph" } ]
          } ],
        "night_min_temp": "0", "temp_unit": "c"
      } ]
  }
}
```

```
var jobj := web→download json(
  "http://www.myweather2.com/developer/forecast.ashx?uac=X&
  output=json&query=SW1")
```

It will download JSON data similar to that shown in Figure 4-6. (The 'X' shown after 'uac=' in the URL must be replaced by a user access code which is given to you only if you register with the weather2 website.)

The value retrieved by this API call has the data type Json Object. The data type provides many methods for accessing information from inside a JSON object. These methods are listed in Appendix C. Using these methods, here is how we could obtain today's temperature from the JSON object shown in Figure 4-6. The code is shown as a series of very simple steps.

```
// assume jobj has been read using the call previously shown
if jobj → is invalid then
    "unable to download JSON data" → post to wall
else
    var w := jobj → field("weather")
    var cw := w → field("curren_weather")
    // get first element of array
    var cw0 := cw → at(0)
    // get temperature as a Number
    var temp := cw0 → string("temp") → to number
    // get temperature units as a String
    var units := cw0 → string("temp_unit")
    ("Today's temperature is " || temp || units) → post to wall
```

All we had to do was look at one example of the JSON data produced by our weather query. From that example, it was easy to figure out how to extract the information we needed. (Of course, we could have also read the documentation provided by the service provider.)

Two popular services which provide results in the JSON format are *Flickr* and *Twitter*. Two scripts in the TouchDevelop Samples collections implement libraries for using these services. A trivial script which searches for tweets containing a particular keyword (or #tag) is shown in Figure 4-7.

The code for the library can be found under the name *twitter search* (/stlm). It extracts enough information from each tweet to format it as a message with an author name, a picture of the author, the date when the tweet was posted, plus the message itself.

4.3.2   *Downloading information in XML format*

XML is short for *Extensible Markup Language*. It is a notation for adding markup to a text document so as to show its structure. It provides an alternative to JSON for delivering results from web services in a format which can easily be processed by software and which is moderately easy for a human to read.

Figure 4-7: Accessing Twitter with a library

```
action main ( keyword : String )
do
    var msgs := ⌂twitter search→ search(keyword, false)
    for each msg in msgs
        where true
    do
        msgs → post to wall

import twitter search
published mdvf
```

An incomplete example of the XML produced by the *weather2* service is shown in Figure 4-8. The information is the same as shown in Figure 4-6 but, because it is rather more voluminous, only the first 25 lines are displayed. As seen in the example, the start of a component (a logical unit) in the document is flagged by an opening tag such as <weather>. The end of that component is flagged by a matching close tag such as </weather>. The components can be nested, as seen in the figure.

An opening tag can include attributes, such as this one <font name="Courier" size="12">, though this possibility does not occur in the weather data.

Downloading XML data requires a call to web→download to fetch the data as a string, and then a call to web→xml to parse the string as XML, as in the following example.

```
    var xobj := web→xml( web→download( "http://www.myweather2.com/
developer/forecast.ashx?uac=X&output=xml&query=SW1"))
```

The result of the code is a value with the datatype Xml Object. This datatype provides methods for traversing the XML object and extracting various components. The methods are listed in Appendix C.

Extracting the current temperature from XML shown in Figure 4-8 can be programmed as follows.

Figure 4-8: Weather data in JSON format

```
<weather>
 <curren_weather>
  <temp>6</temp>
  <temp_unit>c</temp_unit>
  <wind>
   <speed>4</speed>
   <dir>ENE</dir>
   <wind_unit>kph</wind_unit>
  </wind>
  <humidity>87</humidity>
  <pressure>1005</pressure>
  <weather_text>Partly cloudy</weather_text>
  <weather_code>1</weather_code>
 </curren_weather>
 <forecast>
  <date>2012-04-14</date>
  <temp_unit>c</temp_unit>
  <day_max_temp>12</day_max_temp>
  <night_min_temp>1</night_min_temp>
  <day>
   <weather_text>Cloudy skies</weather_text>
   <weather_code>2</weather_code>
   <wind>
    <speed>14</speed>
    <dir>NNE</dir>

... another 21 lines have been omitted
```

```
// assume xobj has been read using the call previously shown
if xobj → is invalid then
     "unable to download XML data" → post to wall
else
     var cw := xobj → child("curren_weather")
     // get temperature
     var temp := cw → child("temp") → to string
     // get temperature units
```

```
var units := cw → child("temp_unit") → to string
("Today's temperature is " || temp || units) → post to wall
```

As with JSON, it is fairly easy to figure out how to extract the desired information just by looking at an example of the XML data. However, the structure of the XML is almost always rigidly defined by a DTD (Document Type Definition) which specifies the tag names to use and how they are allowed to nest inside other tagged sections. It is preferable to consult the DTD when developing scripts for processing XML.

4.4   REST guidelines and web requests

Many web services implement those services in a manner which follows guidelines known as REST. It is short for *REpresentational State Transfer*. Such a web service is often described as being RESTful. A starting point for reading about the REST guidelines is provided by Wikipedia at this URL: http://en.wikipedia.org/wiki/REST.

In particular, HTTP GET and POST requests are used to access many of the facilities of a RESTful web service and the API calls provided for uploading and downloading to or from the web may be adequate. The HTTP PUT and DELETE requests are not supported on the Windows Phone platform and therefore cannot be generated by a TouchDevelop script. Many RESTful web services provide alternatives to the PUT and DELETE requests.

The API method web→create request may be used to construct a general HTTP request. The request is constructed as an instance of the Web Request datatype. When the request is sent to the web service, the result comes back as an instance of the Web Response type. The methods of these two datatypes are summarized in Table 4-4 and Table 4-5. (Methods available for all datatypes are omitted from these two tables.)

Table 4-4: Methods of Web Request datatype

Method	Description
header(name : String) : String	Gets the value of a header identified by name
header names : String Collection	Gets the names of all the headers
method : String	Returns the HTML method: "get" or "post"
send : Web Response	Sends the request and waits for a response
set compress(value : Boolean) : Nothing	If the argument is true, the request content is compressed with gzip (and the header is updated).
set content(content : String) : Nothing	Sets the content of a POST request
set content as json(json : Json Object) : Nothing	Sets the content of a POST request as a JSON data structure
set content as picture(picture : Picture, quality : Number) : Nothing	Sets the content of a POST request as a JPEG image; the quality parameter ranges from 0 for low quality (maximum compression) to 1 for best quality.
set content as xml(xml : Xml Object): Nothing	Sets the content of a POST request as an XML data structure
set credentials(name : String, password : String): Nothing	Sets the name and password when the website requires authentication; the URL for the request must specify HTTPS protocol.
set header(name : String, value : String): Nothing	Sets a HTML header value.
set method(method : String) : Nothing	Sets the method; it must be "get" or "post".
set url(url : String) : Nothing	Sets the URL.
url : String	Returns the URL used in this request

An example of constructing a web request and using the response is provided by the script *cosm services* (/ybnr).

Table 4-5: Methods of Web Response datatype

Method	Description
content : String	Gets the content of the response body as a string
content as json : Json Object	Gets the content of the response body as a JSON data structure
content as picture : Picture	Gets the content of the response body as a picture
content as sound : Sound	Gets the content of the response body as a sound in WAV format
content as xml : Xml Object	Gets the content of the response body as an XML structure
header(name : String) : String	Gets value of the HTML header with the given name
header names : String Collection	Gets the names of the headers
request : Web Request	Gets the web request which was used
status code : Number	Gets the HTTP status code associated with the request

Chapter 5
Audio

A smartphone or tablet can double as a portable music player. It can play music held as MP3 files on the device. It can play audio streamed over the internet, it can record sound using its microphone ... and more.

5.1   Music

Music files can be copied onto your device by a variety of means. Music can also be purchased and downloaded onto your device from a variety of on-line services. The supported formats for music files are listed in Table 5-1. If your file is in another format, there are programs available to convert it to a supported format. The names used in the 'container' column of the table are likely to be the same as the filename extensions used in the filenames on the computer (e.g. "track1.mp3"), but this is not guaranteed to be the case.

Table 5-1: Supported music formats

Codec	Container	Notes
AAC	M4A	Only unprotected (DRM-free) files are supported
MP3	MP3	Layer III of MPEG-1 to be precise
WMA	WMA	Zune converts lossless WMA to another format

The TouchDevelop API provides the media resource. However due to security restrictions, many methods of this resource are available only for use on the Windows Phone and on Android devices. On other devices, it is not possible to access song albums or the entire collection of songs held on the device.

On the Windows phone and Android devices, the media resource has methods for retrieving collections of all the songs, all the song albums, and all the playlists held on the phone. TouchDevelop does not provide any mechanism for changing any of these three collections. They are *immutable*. It is therefore impossible for a mistake in a TouchDevelop script to cause any music file on the phone to be accidentally deleted. The three media methods are listed in Table 5-2.

Table 5-2: Accessing media resources (WP8 and Android only)

Method	Description
media→songs : Songs	Gets a collection of all the songs on the phone
media→song albums : Song Albums	Gets a collection of all the song albums on the phone
media→playlists : Playlists	Gets a collection of all the playlists on the phone

5.1.1   *Working with collections of songs*

Although the TouchDevelop documentation and this book use the words 'music' and 'song', the API calls are of course not restricted to working with music. They will work equally well with recordings made in any of the audio formats listed in Table 5-1.

Note that the TouchDevelop API also provides methods for working with audio recordings in the WAV format but these recordings are not usually used for music, they are short in duration, and they are represented in the TouchDevelop API by the Sound datatype. The Sound type is covered later in this chapter.

The methods for using songs, song albums, and playlists are listed in Table 5-3. The is invalid and post to wall methods (available for all datatypes) are omitted from the table.

Table 5-3: Using songs and song albums (WP8 and Android only)

Method of Playlist Datatype	Description
duration : Number	Returns total duration of all songs in the playlist in seconds
name : String	Returns name of the playlist
play : Nothing	Plays all the songs in the playlist
songs : Songs	Gets all the songs in the playlist as a collection
Method of Song Album	**Description**
art : Picture	Gets the album cover art
artist : String	Gets the album artist's name
duration : Number	Gets the total duration of all songs on the album in seconds
genre : String	Gets the music genre
has art : Boolean	Returns true if cover art is available
name : String	Returns the name of the album
play : Nothing	Plays all the songs on the album
songs : Songs	Returns a collection of all songs on the album
thumbnail : Picture	Gets a thumbnail picture of the cover art
album : Song Album	Gets the album in which the song appears
artist : String	Gets the song artist's name
duration : Number	Gets the song duration in seconds
genre : String	Gets the song's music genre
name : String	Gets the name of the song
play : Nothing	Plays the song
play count : Number	Gets the number of times song has been played
Method of Song Datatype	**Description**
protected : Boolean	Returns true if the song is DRM protected
rating : Number	Gets a rating set by the user; -1 if not rated
track: Number	Gets the track number of song on the album

TouchDevelop also provides one event related to songs. This is the active song changed event which is triggered at the moments that its name suggests. For example, an album or a playlist may be in the process of being played, and the event will be triggered whenever the phone advances to the next song in the list.

5.1.2   Obtaining an individual song, available on all devices

It is possible to import an individual music track into a TouchDevelop script, no matter which platform the script is running on.

One possibility is to download a music file from the web. The action

```
var song := web → download song(url)
```

will load the music into the variable song (with type Song), where url is a string giving a URL for the location of the file.

Alternatively, the script can open a choose file dialog where the user can navigate to the music file on their computer or tablet. The usage is as below.

```
var song := media → choose song
```

5.1.3   Playing an individual song

The play method of the Song, Song Album or Playlist types will start a song or a sequence of songs playing on the phone. For example:

```
song → play
```

More precise control over the playing of songs is provided by the player resource in the API. The methods directly related to playing songs are listed in Table 5-4.

Table 5-4: Methods of player resource for songs

Method of player resource	Description
player→active song: Song	Gets the current song, if any
player→is muted : Boolean	Reports whether the player is muted
player→is paused : Boolean	Reports whether current song is paused
player→is playing : Boolean	Reports whether a song is playing
player→is repeating : Boolean	Reports whether song is in repeat mode
player→is shuffled : Boolean	Reports whether the songs are shuffled
player→is stopped : Boolean	Reports if the player is stopped
player→next : Nothing	Stops current song and advances to next one in the queue waiting to be played
player→pause : Nothing	Pauses the current song

player→play(song : Song): Nothing	Adds a song to the queue of songs
player→play many(songs : Songs) : Nothing	Adds all songs in the collection to the queue
player→play position : Number	Gets the position in seconds within the current song
player→previous : Nothing	Stops current song and goes back to the previous one
player→resume : Nothing	Resumes a paused song
player→set repeating(repeating : Boolean) : Nothing	Sets the repeating mode for the current song
player→set shuffled(shuffled : Boolean) : Nothing	Sets shuffling on or off for songs in the queue
player→set sound volume(x : Number) : Nothing	Sets the sound volume: 0.0 is silent, 1.0 is the volume when TouchDevelop started
player→sound volume : Number	Gets the sound volume in the same 0 to 1 scale
player→stop : Nothing	Stops playing a song
player→volume : Number	Gets player volume, from 0.0 (silence) to 1.0 (full volume).

When an album or a playlist is sent to the player, the player creates a queue of songs to be played. The songs will by default be played in the order that they appear in the album or playlist. However a random order will be used if shuffle is selected. Requesting a new song to be played before the current song is finished causes the current song to be terminated and the queue to be cleared (if it is not empty) before the new song starts.

Playing songs occurs in the background. This means that the player is performing its task while the device and, perhaps, the TouchDevelop script is doing other things. When a song or collection of songs is given to the player, the player remembers what it has to play and starts playing. Control is returned to the script for it to carry on executing statements while the music is playing.

The playing volume ranges from 0.0 to 1.0. The value of 1.0 does not correspond to the maximum volume which the device is capable of. The value is relative to the volume of the player as set externally to the TouchDevelop script. A script cannot play songs louder than the device's current setting, but it can play at a quieter level by using a value less than 1.0

for the volume.

5.1.4   An example script

There are many example programs on the TouchDevelop website which select and play music. One sample program for the Windows Phone and Android platforms is reproduced below in Figure 5-1. It uses several features provided by the API.

There is one feature of this script that is not obvious when reading it. When it is run, it will display information about each song on the phone which has never been previously played. If the user scrolls through the list of displayed songs and taps one, it will immediately start playing.

Figure 5-1: The 'new songs' script (WP8 and Android only)

```
action main( )
  // Finds songs not played yet.
  var found := 0
  var songs := media→♫songs
  for each song in songs where true
  do
     found := found + ▷display song(song)
  ("Songs played with this script: " ‖ ▣played) → post to wall
  ("Songs never played: " ‖ found) → post to wall

action display song(song : Song) returns result : Number
  // Post a song to the wall if not played yet and returns 1;
  // otherwise returns 0.
  if song → play count = 0 then
     song → post to wall
     result := 1
  else
     result := 0

event active song changed
  // Increment the song played counter.
  ▣played := ▣played + 1

event shake
  // Pauses and resumes playing.
  if player → is playing then
     player → pause
  else
     player → resume
```

5.2   Sounds

The Sound datatype is used for audio recordings in the WAV format. This format is commonly used for uncompressed audio and therefore the files tend to be large. This format should therefore be used only for short sound clips (say 30 seconds or less), such as ring tones, sound effects or warning noises to be played by your script. For longer pieces, the Song datatype and therefore a compressed sound format should be used, if possible.

The Sound datatype provides many methods for playing the sound clip and altering its properties when played. These are summarized in Table 5-5.

Panning refers to the ability to choose whether the sound should be played wholly through the left earpiece or wholly through the right earpiece or through both together in some proportion. The pan value ranges from -1.0 for fully left to 0.0 for center (i.e. both sides equally) to 1.0 for fully right.

Table 5-5: Methods of Sound datatype

Method of Sounds	Description
duration : Number	Returns the sound clip's duration in seconds
pan : Number	Gets the pan setting: from -1 for full left to +1 for right
play : Nothing	Plays the sound clip
play special(volume : Number, pitch : Number, pan : Number) : Nothing	Plays the sound clip with values supplied for the panning, pitch and volume
pitch : Number	Gets the pitch adjustment from -1 to +1
set pan(pan : Number) : Nothing	Sets the pan setting: from -1 for full left to +1 for right
set pitch(pitch : Number) : Nothing	Sets the pitch adjustment from -1 to +1
set volume(v : Number) : Nothing	Sets the volume from 0 (silent) to +1 (full volume)
volume : Number	Gets the volume, in range 0 (silent) to +1 (full volume)

The pitch adjustment ranges from -1.0 to 1.0. If -1.0 is selected, the playback speed is slowed down so that the pitch is lowered by one octave. The midpoint value 0.0 plays the sound clip at normal speed. The top value of 1.0 causes playback to speeded up so that the pitch is raised by one octave.

As with playing Song values, the volume is a value ranging from 0.0 to 1.0 where 1.0 is the current volume setting for the speakers as set externally of the TouchDevelop script. The script can play sounds at a quieter level than this setting but it cannot play them louder.

5.3   Microphone

Most devices have a microphone. However, the microphone cannot be accessed from a program running in a browser on a PC, Mac or Linux platform. It can be accessed on the Windows phone and the ability to access it will be supported on iPad, iPhone, iPod Touch and Android platforms in the near future.

The TouchDevelop API provides a method for activating the microphone and making a recording.

```
var snd := senses → record microphone
// snd has the datatype Sound
```

When the above statement is executed in a script, the word "Recording..." and a stop button are displayed on the screen. Simultaneously, the microphone begins recording. When the user taps the stop button, recording stops and an instance of the Sound datatype is returned.

As noted earlier, a Sound value uses the WAV audio format and is not compressed. Therefore the microphone should not be used for long recordings.

Chapter 6
Camera, Graphics and Video

A smartphones, tablets and laptops are commonly used for displaying photographs and videos. TouchDevelop scripts provide new ways to download, create, modify and display photographs. Scripts can be used to record videos using the device's camera and to play back both those videos and videos obtained from elsewhere.

6.1   Camera

Smartphones, tablets and most laptops have at least one camera capable of taking high-quality pictures or videos. This is the *primary camera*. On a phone or tablet, it would normally be located on the opposite side from the screen. Many of these devices have a second camera located above the screen which captures the user's image and is intended for use in video calls, such as a Skype call. A camera above the screen is normally the only one provided on a laptop, and would be considered to be the primary camera by TouchDevelop.

The TouchDevelop API provides access to the camera (or cameras) via its senses service. The senses methods relevant to using the cameras are listed in Table 6-1. Two of these methods return instances of type Camera. This datatype provides methods for retrieving information about the camera and for taking a quick low-quality picture on a smartphone.

Table 6-1: Methods for using the camera(s)

Method	Description
senses → camera: Camera	Returns the primary camera, if there is one; otherwise the result is invalid.
senses → front camera: Camera	Returns the secondary camera, if there is one; otherwise the result is *invalid.*
senses → take camera picture: Picture	Uses the primary camera to take a picture.
wall → set background camera(camera: Camera): Nothing	Causes images from the selected camera to be used as the background for the wall

There are two ways to take a picture with the primary camera. The two approaches behave differently on a phone, but will normally behave identically on a laptop or tablet. The two forms are

senses → take camera picture

and

senses → front camera → preview

On a Windows phone, the first form takes a high-resolution picture using the phone's built-in software. This causes a preview image to appear on the screen along with controls for adjusting the zoom level, exposure and flash etc. Control is not returned to the TouchDevelop script until the button to take the picture has been pressed and the picture taken. The second form just returns the preview image without any delay. On other devices, the two forms will both take pictures almost immediately and with the same resolution. The user may be prompted to allow or deny the script access to the camera.

All methods (except for invalid and post to wall) are listed in Table 6-2.

The user has the option of cancelling the picture capture in the high-quality version on a phone. Therefore the normal pattern of usage in a script might be code like the following. (An audible warning, such as beeps, to indicate when the picture is about to be snapped would be a useful addition to the script.)

```
"You have three seconds!" → post to wall
// give 3 seconds for user to get ready
time → sleep(3)
var pic := senses → take camera picture
if not pic → is invalid then
    // use the picture pic

    ...
else
    // user cancelled the picture
```

To determine whether the device has a secondary camera, a script should invoke the senses → front camera method. (The name of this method is perhaps inappropriate for a laptop or PC.) If the result is the invalid value, then this camera is absent.

Table 6-2: Methods of the Camera datatype

Method	Description
height : Number	Returns the height of the camera image in pixels.
is front : Boolean	Returns true if this is the secondary camera, false if this is the primary camera.
preview : Picture	Takes a low quality picture with the camera, returning the picture immediately.
width : Number	Returns the width of the camera image in pixels.

6.1.1   A sample program

The script *the poor man's camcorder* (/ptxfa) asks you to sweep the camera slowly around while it takes 10 pictures in succession using the preview method of the Camera type. It then plays back the 10 pictures, giving the effect of a camcorder whose recordings are 2 seconds long.

A simplified and reprogrammed version of this script is presented in Figure 6-1.

This sample program also illustrates the use of an **object** declaration in the

Records section of a script. It is used to create a data structure known as a *cyclic list*. It is a linked-list where every element of the list contains a reference to the next element, except that the last element references the first element, creating a cycle.

Figure 6-1: A simplified camcorder script (/xbhl)

```
action main( number of pics: Number )
   // number of pics is the number of pictures to take and
   //  display repeatedly; the recommended value is 10
   if number of pics ≤ 0 then
      number of pics := 10
   else
      // do nothing
   var camera := senses → camera
   var firstpic  := ⊞PicList → create
   firstpic → pic → set( camera → preview )
   var prev := firstpic
   for 0 ≤ i < number of pics – 1 do
      var newpic := ⊞PicList → create
      newpic → pic → set( camera → preview )
      prev → next → set(newpic)
      prev := newpic
   // Make last pic in list point to first pic, i.e. a cyclic list
   prev → next → set(firstpic)
   // Go around the cyclic list forever
   prev := firstpic
   while true do
      wall → clear
      prev → pic → get → post to wall
      time → sleep( 0.2 )
      prev := prev → next → get

object PicList
fields
   pic: Picture
   next: PicList
```

6.2   Working with pictures

6.2.1   *Picture albums and picture collections (Windows Phone and Android)*

A smartphone normally holds various picture albums. On a Windows phone, they have names such as *Camera Roll* and *Saved Favorites*.

TouchDevelop provides access to these albums on the Windows Phone and will soon provide access to picture albums on Android devices. Unfortunately, security restrictions prevent access on the PC, Mac, Linux, iPad, iPhone and iPod Touch platforms.

On the platforms where it is supported, the API call

phone → picture albums

retrieves all the albums currently maintained on the phone, while the two method calls

phone → pictures
phone → saved pictures

return collections of all pictures, and the pictures held in the album named 'saved pictures', respectively. The methods for working with the Picture Album, Picture Albums and Pictures (a Picture collection) datatypes are listed in Table 6-3.

Once a Picture value has been obtained, perhaps by retrieving it from a collection, or by using the camera, there are many methods for manipulating the picture before it is displayed on the screen. These are covered in later sections of this chapter.

Table 6-3: Methods of Picture Album and Pictures Datatypes (WP8 and Android)

Methods of Picture Album Datatype	Description
albums : Picture Albums	Returns a collection of all the nested albums held inside this album.
name : String	Obtains the name of the album.
pictures : Pictures	Returns a collection of all the pictures held in the album.
Methods of Pictures Datatype	**Description**
find(name : String) : Number	Returns the index of a picture in the collection which has the given name; the result is -1 if the picture cannot be found.
random : Picture	Returns a random picture.
thumbnail(index : Number) : Picture	Returns a thumbnail of the picture at the given index position in the collection.

6.2.2   Access to pictures on other devices

In the Web App version of TouchDevelop, a single picture can be selected from the device's hard drive using the method media → choose picture. A picture can also be downloaded from the web via the call

```
Var pic := web →  choose picture
```

or added to a script as an Art resource.

6.2.3   Manipulating a picture

Display of an image uses the post to wall method, as in this example.

```
var pic1 := media → choose picture
pic1 → post to wall
```

An alternative way to display a picture is to set the wall's background image, as follows.

```
var pic1 := media → choose picture
wall → set background picture(pic1)
```

The general-purpose methods of the Picture type are listed in Table 6-4.

Table 6-4: General Picture methods

Methods of Picture Datatype	Description
at(index: Number): Color	Returns the color of the pixel at the given index in the picture
clone : Picture	Returns a copy of the Picture
count : Number	Returns number of pixels
crop(left : Number, top : Number, width : Number, height : Number)	Crops the picture to a rectangular portion of the original.
date : DateTime	Returns a date associated with the picture (if there is one)
flip horizontal	flips the picture left to right
flip vertical	flips the picture top to bottom
height : Number	Returns height of picture in pixels
is panorama : Boolean	Returns true if width > height
location : Location	Returns a location associated with the picture (if there is one)
pixel(left : Number, top : Number) : Color	Gets the pixel color at the specified x,y position
post to wall	Displays the picture
resize(width : Number, height : Number)	Scales the picture to have a new width and height
save to library : String	Stores the picture in the Saved Pictures album and returns the filename
set pixel(left : Number, top : Number, color : Color)	Sets the pixel color at the specified x,y position
update on wall	If this picture has been displayed and then changed, this method replaces the displayed image with the new one
width : Number	Returns width of picture in pixels

The table omits methods which change the colors or the brightness, or methods which overlay shapes etc. on top of the picture. All such methods are covered in the following subsections of this chapter.

Care in Using the at, pixel and set pixel methods

Table 6-4 includes the at, pixel and set pixel methods. Before any of these methods is used in a script, some thought should be given to how large the picture is.

Any TouchDevelop script which accesses every pixel of a picture can be exceedingly slow to run, as well as draining the battery of a portable device. The implication is that the Picture type's at, pixel and set pixel methods should be used only on pictures containing a modest number of pixels. Pictures taken by the camera contain as many pixels as the camera's resolution. For example, it is not uncommon for phone cameras to have 6 megapixel resolution or higher. Pictures downloaded from the internet or transferred from your computer may contain even more pixels.

Although a picture shown on the screen is scaled to fit within the screen's size, the picture retains its original number of pixels in the device's memory. Unless the picture is intended to be copied to another device, it would usually be appropriate to reduce the picture's resolution to match the screen resolution. Note that any method which processes all the pixels in a single call, such as resize, is reasonably fast.

The at method is useful for determining various aggregate properties of a picture, such as its average brightness. In more sophisticated scripts, the pixel method could for example be used for analyzing a picture and extracting details such as edges or, when set pixel is used too, for sharpening edges.

An example script which computes a picture's average brightness is shown in Figure 6-2. Each pixel in the picture has a color value composed from red (R), green (G) and blue (B) components whose values range from zero intensity or 0.0 up to the maximum intensity which is 1.0. From the R,G,B values of a pixel, its luminosity can be calculated. (See, for example, the explanation of the YUV color space and the conversion formula for computing YUV values in Wikipedia.) The luminosity is a measure of the brightness of that pixel.

Figure 6-2: Computing brightness

```
// use this only for low resolution pictures!
action compute brightness( pic : Picture ) returns avg y : Number
    var sum y := 0
    for 0 ≤ i < pic → count do
        var c := pic → at(i)
        // compute y = luminosity of pixel (i.e. brightness level)
        var y := c → R * 0.299 + c → G * 0.587 + c → B * 0.114
        sum y := sum y + y
    avg y := sum y / pic→ count
```

The at and pixel methods are similar because they both retrieve the color of a particular pixel. Generally speaking, the at method should be used when it does not matter where the pixel is located within the picture, as is the case for the brightness calculation in Figure 6-2. It provides more efficient access because only one for loop to access all the pixels is needed. The pixel and set pixel methods would normally be placed inside two nested for loops, one to run through the rows and the other through the columns. The equivalence between the two ways to access a particular pixel is as follows.

$$\text{pic1} \rightarrow \text{pixel(x,y)} \quad \equiv \quad \text{pic1} \rightarrow \text{at(y*pic1} \rightarrow \text{width + x)}$$

Note that y coordinate values are measured from the top edge of the picture down. It is the opposite convention to that used in geometry.

Picture colorizing effects

The colors, the contrast and the brightness of a picture can all be modified using more methods of the Picture type which are listed in Table 6-5.

The brightness method can be used to increase or decrease the luminosities of all the pixels in the image in unison, so that the picture appears brighter or darker. The contrast method can be used to increase or decrease the range of luminosities, so that there is greater or smaller contrast between light and dark regions.

The colorize method is intended for creating a two color image from a greyscale image. All pixels darker than a specified threshold value (a number in the range 0.0 to 1.0) are replaced by the background color, while all those brighter are replaced by the foreground color. The method can also be applied to color images, but that image is converted to grayscale before the colorization is applied.

Table 6-5: Colorizing/intensity picture effects

Methods of Picture	Description
brightness(factor : Number) : Nothing	Increases of decreases the brightness of the picture. The parameter ranges from -1 to +1.
colorize(background : Color, foreground : Color, threshold : Number) : Nothing	Changes the picture to a two color scheme. Pixels darker than threshold become the background color, those brighter become the foreground color.
contrast(factor : Number) : Nothing	Increases or decreases contrast level of the picture. The parameter ranges from -1 to +1.
desaturate : Nothing	Converts the picture to grayscale.
invert : Nothing	Inverts the intensity of each of the R, G, B color components
tint(color : Color) : Nothing	Converts the picture to grayscale, and then tints with the supplied color

The final picture will no longer have any variations in intensity. All pixels of the foreground color have the same intensity, as do all those with the background color.

The invert method produces a result similar to a color negative, as would be observed with a 35mm camera using chemically developed color film. (This is a type of camera which is becoming rare.)

Picture overlaying

The next section in this chapter, section 6.3, is all about drawing text, lines and various shapes on top of a picture. What about superimposing another picture on top of a picture? That facility is provided by the blend method. It is called *blend* as opposed to 'superimpose' say, because one of the method's parameters chooses the opacity of the overlaid image. By choosing a low degree of opacity, the image at the bottom can be seen through the image on the top – achieving a blending of the two images.

The following few lines of code illustrate the concept.

```
var pic1 := media → choose picture
var w := pic1 → width
var h := pic1 → height
var pic2 := media → choose picture
pic2 → resize( w*0.5, h*0.5 )
pic1 → blend( pic2, w*0.3, h*0.2, 30, 0.7 )
pic1 → post to wall
```

The relationship of the two pictures to each other is illustrated in Figure 6-3.

Figure 6-3: Blending two pictures

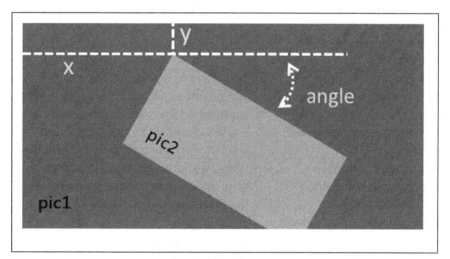

The top left corner of pic2 is located at the x,y coordinates given by the second and third arguments to blend. This picture is rotated clockwise by the number of degrees given by the fourth argument. The opacity of the picture has been set at 0.7, which means that in the overlaid region, each pixel is a blend of 70% from pic2 and 30% from pic1. Finally, the bottom right of pic2 has been clipped to fit within pic1.

6.3   Static graphics drawing and display

A picture can be a photograph, a drawing, or a combination of the two. The methods provided by the Picture datatype for drawing lines and shapes are listed in Table 6-6.

Table 6-6: Drawing methods of the Picture datatype

Methods of Picture	Description
clear(color : Color)	Sets all pixels to the given color
draw ellipse(left: Number, top: Number, width: Number, height : Number, angle : Number, c: Color, thickness: Number)	Draws an ellipse; its bounding rectangle has the given width and height and is located at the specified position; its orientation is rotated clockwise by the angle given; the line has the color and thickness specified.
draw line(x1: Number, y1: Number, x2: Number, y2: Number, color: Color, thickness : Number)	Draws a line from x1,y1 to x2,y2; the line has the color and thickness specified.
draw rect(left : Number, top : Number, width : Number, height : Number, angle : Number, c : Color, thickness : Number)	Draws a rectangle which has the width and height provided and is located at the specified position; its orientation is rotated clockwise by the angle given; the line has the color and thickness specified.
draw text(left : Number, top : Number, text : String, font size : Number, angle : Number, color : Color)	Writes text at the position specified, at the given font size and in the specified color; the text is rotated clockwise by the angle given
fill ellipse(left : Number, top : Number, width : Number, height : Number, angle : Number, color : Color)	Like draw ellipse except that it is a solid (filled) ellipse.
fill rect(left : Number, top : Number, width : Number, height : Number, angle : Number, color : Color)	Like draw rect except that it is a solid (filled) rectangle.

In addition to these, there is the set pixel method which has already been covered and also the create picture method of the media resource for creating a new empty picture as illustrated below. All pixels in the new picture are colored white.

```
// create picture 400 pixels wide, 200 pixels high
var pic := media → create picture( 400, 200 )
```

Figure 6-4 shows how the parameters of the draw ellipse method control the placement and orientation of the ellipse within a picture. An ellipse fits within a bounding rectangle, as drawn, and it is the width and height of that rectangle which are specified as arguments of the method.

Figure 6-4: Using the draw ellipse method

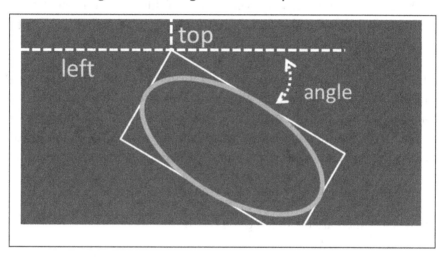

The left and top parameters provide the x, y coordinates of the top left corner of that bounding rectangle. Note that y coordinate values are measured downwards from the top of the picture.

A circle is a special case of an ellipse. Most graphics drawing software would draw a circle of a given radius and with its center at a specified position. To use the draw ellipse method, some extra arithmetic is needed. An action which accepts radius and the position of the center would be programmed as follows.

```
// Draws a circle with radius r and center at x, y.
action Draw Circle( pic: Picture, r: Number, x: Number, y: Number,
           thickness: Number, color: Color )
    pic → draw ellipse( x-r, y-r, r*2, r*2, 0, color, thickness )
```

Drawing rectangles and filled versions of ellipses and rectangles is handled similarly; further explanation should not be needed.

6.4   Playing videos from the internet

Video files tend to be very large. You should think before storing one on a device with limited memory, such as a phone. Videos held on the phone can be created by using the phone's camera or by being copied from a PC when the phone is synchronized.

TouchDevelop does not provide access to video files held on a smartphone. Nor can a script download a video file to the phone. However a script can access and play videos which are streamed from the internet.

Given the URL of a video file which is in a format that the device can play, a TouchDevelop script can open and play that file. The supported video formats can depend on the particular model of device in use. However most video files with the filename suffix '.mp4' should work. (An H.264 encoded MP4 file is the format which works on every Windows phone, for example.)

Given the URL, a direct way to play the video is as follows.

```
// url is a String variable holding the URL of the file
web → play media( url )
```

It displays the video using the entire window. The back button can be used to stop the video.

An alternative means of playing the video is to create a Link value. Some sample code is as follows.

```
// url is a String variable holding the URL of the file
var lnk := web → link media( url )
...
if not lnk → is invalid then
      lnk → post to wall
      "Tap video link to play it" → post to wall
else
      ("Could not access url " || url) → post to wall
```

The second approach shown above allows a script to show a list of links on the screen, allowing the user to select which one to play.

Chapter 7
Sensors

A typical smartphone or tablet contains sensors which track the device's location, movement and orientation. Scripts can use these sensors in many ways. Sensors can provide input for navigation aids, they can be an integral part of a game, and they can provide simple input to scripts. The possibilities are endless. These sensors are probably absent from laptops and computers, however.

7.1   The sensors

The full complement of sensors supported by TouchDevelop may not be available on your device. The possible sensors are as follows.

- *GPS* (Global Positioning System), which obtains the phone's current location on the map.
- *Accelerometer*, which measures gravitational and acceleration forces experienced by the phone.
- *Compass*, which returns the direction of magnetic north.
- *Gyroscope*, which measures the phone's orientation in 3D space.

A script's access to the sensors is provided by calls to a variety of API methods and by events associated with the gyroscope and accelerometer. The API methods are listed in Table 7-1; the events are listed in Table 7-2.

Table 7-1: Sensing methods of the senses service

Accelerometer Methods	Description
senses → acceleration quick : Vector3	Returns an acceleration averaged over a short time interval
senses → acceleration smooth : Vector3	Returns an acceleration averaged over a moderate time interval
senses → acceleration stable : Vector3	Returns an acceleration averaged over a time interval of about 0.5 seconds
senses → is device stable : Boolean	Returns true if the phone has not moved for about 0.5 seconds
Compass Methods	**Description**
senses → heading : Number	Returns the angle in degrees of magnetic north compared to the direction that the phone is facing
Gyroscope Methods	**Description**
senses → has gyroscope : Boolean	Returns true if the phone has a gyroscope
senses → orientation : Vector3	Obtains the current orientation in degrees with respect to the X, Y, Z axes, if available.
senses → rotation speed : Vector3	Returns the rotational speed in degrees per second about each of the X, Y, Z axes
Motion Methods	**Description**
senses → motion : Boolean	Returns the phone's current motion, combining readings from accelerometer, compass and gyroscope

7.2   Sensor-driven events

If the device is shaken, the accelerometer records some rapidly changing readings. If the amplitude of the shaking exceeds a certain threshold, a shake event is triggered. A script can use the event to effect an action, such as pausing the playback of an audio recording.

The device's software may be using the gyroscope to determine the screen's orientation, and so to choose between portrait mode or landscape mode for presentation of information. Several possibilities for the orientation can be transmitted to a TouchDevelop script via the event mechanism.

The shake event and the phone orientation events are listed in Table 7-2.

Table 7-2: Sensor events

Event	Description
shake	Triggered when the phone is shaken
phone face up	Triggered when the device is turned so that it is face up
phone face down	Triggered when the device is turned so that it is face down
phone portrait	Triggered when the device is turned so the screen in portrait mode (such as when the device is vertical)
phone landscape left	Triggered when the device is turned so that its left side is facing down
phone landscape right	Triggered when the device is turned so that its right side is facing down

7.2.1 Example script: A pedometer (/jbpv)

If you carry your smartphone with you when jogging or walking briskly, the phone's sensors should trigger a shake event for each step taken. A simple script can record how many steps are taken, from which the number of steps per minute can be computed. By accessing the GPS location, the average speed can be determined too. However the script cannot simply use the starting location and ending location to determine the distance traveled, because that would give only the straight line distance between the two points. Determining the actual distance traveled requires checking the GPS location more frequently and summing lots of little distances.

The code for a simple Pedometer program is shown in Figure 7-1. Note that you will need to enable *Location Services* in TouchDevelop's settings for the script to work.

7.3   Accelerometer

Most Windows phones possess a device which measures the forces on a small mass. When the phone is held perfectly still, the only force will be gravity. If the phone is shaken or moved, the forces which are measured will combine acceleration with gravity. The measuring device is therefore known as an *accelerometer*.

Gravitational force is always down, towards the ground. However, acceleration can be in any direction in three dimensional space. The accelerometer therefore returns a vector to show the current force in each of the three dimensions. In the TouchDevelop API, that vector is provided as a value with the Vector3 datatype.

Figure 7-1: A simple pedometer program (/jbpv)

```
action main( )
  ⊞steps := 0
  ⊞start time := time → now
  ⊞total distance := 0
  ⊞prev location := senses → current_location
  if ⊞prev location → is invalid then
      "You must enable Location Services for TouchDevelop"
        → post to wall
      time → stop and close
  else  // do nothing
event shake( )
  ⊞steps := ⊞steps + 1
  var dt := time → now
  var elapsed := dt → subtract(⊞start time)
  var curr loc := senses → current location
  var distance := curr loc → distance(⊞prev location)
  ⊞prev location := curr loc
  ⊞total distance := ⊞total distance + math → abs(distance)
  if elapsed > 0 then
      var pace := math → round with precision(⊞steps * 60 / elapsed, 2)
      ("Pace = " ‖ pace ‖ " steps/minute") → post to wall
  else  // do nothing
  if ⊞total distance > 0 then
      var speed := math → round with precision(
          ⊞total distance * 0.36 / elapsed, 2)
      ("Speed = " ‖ speed ‖ " km/hour") → post to wall
  else  // do nothing

data steps : Number          // step counter
data start time : DateTime   // when script started
data total distance : Number // total distance in meters
data prev location : Location  // last recorded location
```

The senses methods which access the accelerometer are listed in Table 7-1. Three methods are provided for finding the phone's acceleration. They are necessary because nothing in real life is perfectly motionless. Any sound or vibration induces small high frequency accelerations in an object. Obtaining steady repeatable readings requires averaging out the measurements over a period of time. Longer periods of time will yield very consistent measurements, but the script has to wait until that period has elapsed before a reading is available.

Long waits would be inappropriate for a game where the player is controlling the actions by moving the phone. Note that the accelerations measured by these three methods include gravitational force. A value of (0.0, 0.0, 0.0) for the acceleration vector could only mean that the phone is in free fall.

7.3.1   Direction of acceleration forces

The three components of a Vector3 value are accessed via the three methods x, y and z. They correspond to the X, Y and Z dimensions, as in Figure 7-2.

As can be seen in the figure, when the phone is lying flat on the table, the vector has a value of the form (0.0, 0.0, k) where k is some negative number. The value of k depends on what units are used for measuring a force. The TouchDevelop API reports the force in g (gravitational) units. Any object which is perfectly stationary is subjected to a force of 1g in the downwards direction. In other words, the Vector3 value returned by the accelerometer should be exactly (0.0, 0.0, -1.0) when the phone is kept still and lying flat on a table with the screen facing up.

When the phone is held vertically with its bottom edge on the table, the Vector3 value should be (0.0, -1.0, 0.0). If we turn the phone upside-down so that the top edge is on the table, the value should be (0.0, 1.0, 0.0).

A short script to show the values of these components is the following.

```
action main( )
    var acc := senses → acceleration quick
    ("Z component = " || acc → z) → post to wall
    ("Y component = " || acc → y) → post to wall
    ("X component = " || acc → x) → post to wall
```

Figure 7-2: Accelerometer orientation

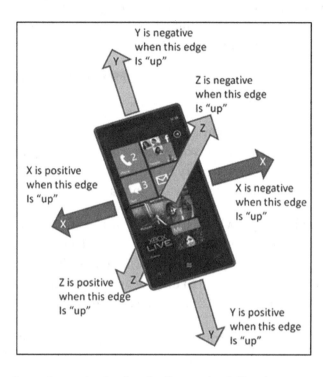

Typical output from the script looks similar to the following:

```
X component = 0.0092241987586021423
Y component = -0.03411596268415451
Z component = -0.99446910619735718
```

The values are close to 0.0, 0.0 and -1.0. The discrepancies show that the accelerometer may have some measuring error and that the phone is probably not located on a perfectly horizontal surface.

7.3.2   Example script: a light show (/tbcb)

This script simply converts movements of the phone into colors, and these colors are applied to the entire screen. The script is shown in Figure 7-3.

The script maps the X, Y and Z components of an acceleration reading to three color components. However it is not a simple mapping. The script needs to ensure that the three color components are kept within the 0.0 to 1.0 range. Secondly, the RGB components of a color do not have equal importance to the human eye. A normal eye is much less responsive to the color blue than to red or green. To distribute the perceived colors out a bit more evenly among the possibilities, an alternative color representation known as HSB (short for *hue, saturation* and *brightness*) is used.

The script takes a reading from the accelerometer every 0.1 seconds and uses it to set the screen's color.

An equivalent version of this script is published on the TouchDevelop website as /wnny. The wnny script uses the gameloop event to trigger a reading of the accelerometer every 50 milliseconds, and it calls an action in a library script to convert a Vector3 value into a Color value.

Another sample script which uses the accelerometer is the simplified airplane attitude indicator, published as /akgk. The current orientation of the phone with respect to gravity is determined by checking the result from the accelerometer. That is used to display an artificial horizon on the screen, simulating what a pilot would see with an attitude indicator in an airplane.

Figure 7-3: Accelerometer colors simplified (script /tbcb)

```
action main( )
  // This is a simplified version of script /wnny
  var board := media → create full board
  board → post to wall
  while true do
    var p := senses → acceleration smooth
    var hue := math → min(math → abs(p → x), 1.0)
    var saturation := math → min(math → abs(p → y), 1.0)
    var brightness := math → min(math → abs(p → z), 1.0)
    var c := colors → from hsb(hue, saturation, brightness)
    board → set background( c )
    board → update on wall
    time → sleep(0.1)
```

7.4   Compass

Most smartphones contain a built-in compass which reports the phone's orientation with respect to magnetic north. The methods of the senses resource which directly use the compass are listed in Table 7-1.

7.4.1   *Example script: a magnetic compass (/drvu)*

As a demonstration of the usage of the compass sensor, the script provided below simulates an old-fashioned magnetic compass, where the compass's needle always points north.

Most of the script is concerned with displaying an arrow, which represents the needle, on top of a solid circle which represents the dial. The important statement in the script concerned with the sensor is the following.

```
var angle := senses → heading  // get heading in degrees
```

The value returned by senses→heading is, as the API documentation says, "the compass heading, in degrees, measured clockwise from the Earth's magnetic north". A value of 15, say, means that the magnetic north should be 15 degrees to the left of the direction in which the phone is currently pointing.

The script is shown in Figure 7-. Most of the code is concerned with drawing a representation of a large arrow.

7.5   Gyroscope

Many Windows phones also possess a gyroscope. This is a device which reports on whether the phone is being rotated – rotated in absolutely any orientation. Rotation is measured as an angular velocity, which is rotation speed in degrees per second about an axis in three dimensional space. The API methods to access the gyroscope are listed in Table 7-1.

The angular velocity is reported by the TouchDevelop API as a Vector3 value reporting rotation in three dimensional space. A value of (360, 0, 0) indicates a rotational speed of one revolution per second about the X axis in a clockwise direction, and similarly for the Y and Z axes. Given a reading of (a, b, c), the combined rotational speed can be computed as $\sqrt{(a^2 + b^2 + c^2)}$ measured about some axis in 3D space.

The value returned by the rotation speed method measures which axis the phone is being rotated about, and how fast. For example, if the X and Y components of the angular velocity are much smaller than the Z component, then the phone is likely to be lying flat on a table and being spun around (because the Z axis is perpendicular to the phone's screen).

Figure 7-4: Magnetic compass script (script /drvu)

```
action main( )
  if senses → heading → is invalid  then
    "Sorry, your phone does not have a compass!" → post to wall
    time → stop
  else  // do nothing
  var hdw := 70   // width of arrow head
  var shw := 30   // width of arrow shaft
  var shl := 300   // length of arrow shaft
  var diam := shl + hdw + 10   // diameter of compass dial
  ▢board := media → create full board
  ▷setBackground(diam)
  ▷createArrow*hdw, shw, shl)
  ▷updateDirection(0)
```

```
action createArrow(hdw: Number, shw: Number, shl: Number)
  var hde := hdw * math → sqrt(2) * 0.5
  ▢tip := ▢board → create rectangle(hde, hde)
  ▢tip → set color(colors → black)
  ▢mask := ▢board → create rectangle(hdw, shl)
  ▢mask → set color(colors → yellow)
  ▢shaft := ▢board → create rectangle(shw, shl)
  ▢shaft → set color(colors → black)
```

```
action updateDirection(angle: Number)
  var d := ▢shaft → height * 0.5
  var x := d * math → sin(math → deg to rad(angle))
  var y := d * math → cos(math → deg to rad(angle))
  ▢tip → set pos(240 + x, 400 - y)
  ▢tip → set angle(45 + angle)
  var mh := ▢mask → height * 0.5
  ▢mask → set pos(240, 400)
  ▢mask → set angle(angle)
  ▢shaft → set pos(240, 400)
  ▢shaft → set angle(angle)
```

```
action setBackground(diam: Number)
  ⊞board → set background(colors → light_gray)
  ⊞board → post to wall
  var dial := ⊞board → create ellipse(diam, diam)
  dial → set color(colors → yellow)
  dial → set pos(240, 400)
  var N := ⊞board → create text(20, 20, 40, "N")
  var S := ⊞board → create text(20, 20, 40, "S")
  var E := ⊞board → create text(20, 20, 40, "E")
  var W := ⊞board → create text(20, 20, 40, "W")
  N → set pos(240, 400 - diam * 0.5 - 50)
  S → set pos(240, 400 + diam * 0.5 + 15)
  W → set pos(240 - diam * 0.5 - 35, 400 - 20)
  E → set pos(240 + diam * 0.5 + 15, 400 - 20)
  N → set color(colors → black)
  S → set color(colors → black)
  E → set color(colors → black)
  W → set color(colors → black)
  ⊞info := ⊞board → create text(200, 20, 20, "")
  ⊞info → set text("MAGNETIC COMPASS")
  ⊞info → set pos(100, 100)
  ⊞info → set angle(0)
  ⊞info → set color(colors→black)
```

```
event gameloop() {
  var angle := senses → heading
  ▷updateDirection( - angle )
  ⊞board → update on wall
```

```
data board : Board
data tip : Sprite     // tip of arrow
data mask : Sprite   // to cover half of tip's rectangle
data shaft : Sprite  // shaft of arrow
data info : Sprite    // the caption displayed at the top
```

7.6   Motion

Perhaps there is a use for gyroscope readings in a game which requires spinning the device around? However, it is much more likely that the gyroscope is useful when used in combination with the accelerometer and compass. The following code snippet extracts a combined reading from all three sensors.

```
var motion := senses → motion
if motion → is invalid then
     "Your device does not have motion capability!" → post to wall
     time →stop
else  // do nothing
```

The value obtained in the first statement has the Motion datatype. Methods associated with the Motion datatype allow various component readings to be extracted. The methods provided by the Motion type are summarized in Figure 7-5 (The is invalid and post to wall methods are omitted).

One very important feature is that the software can separate the force on the accelerometer into the force caused by gravity and the additional force caused by acceleration. In other words, the acceleration method returns a true acceleration and does not include a gravitational force component. The force of gravity should always be equal to 1g but its direction depends on which way the device is oriented.

Another important feature of a Motion value is that an accurate value for the device's orientation can be obtained for the time when the value was captured. The direction of the Vector3 value returned by senses→acceleration quick would usually be adequate, but it can be disturbed by waving the device around. The true orientation of the device is known as its *attitude*. The three methods named pitch, roll and yaw report the phone's attitude measured in degrees, respectively relative to three orthogonal axes. These axes are diagrammed in Figure 7-6 if your smartphone is substituted for the plane. If the phone is held vertically and facing magnetic north, the values for the yaw, pitch and roll should all be zero. Any rotations relative to that starting position will cause the values to become non-zero.

Figure 7-5: Methods of the Motion type

Method	Description
acceleration : Vector3	Gets the acceleration vector of this reading measured in 1g units
gravity : Vector3	Gets the gravity vector of this reading measured in 1g units
pitch : Number	Gets the pitch of the phone's attitude measured in degrees
roll : Number	Gets the roll of the phone's attitude measured in degrees
rotation speed : Vector3	Gets the rotation speed of the phone
time : DateTime	Gets the time at which the motion was measured
yaw : Number	Gets the yaw of the phone's attitude measured in degrees

Note that the current orientation of the phone can be obtained with the senses→ orientation method.

Figure 7-6: Yaw, pitch and roll

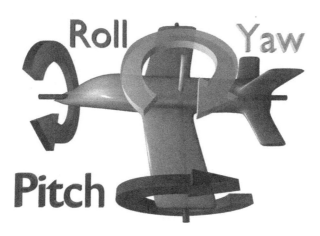

Note: The image has been copied from the Wikipedia Commons, a freely licensed media file repository.

Chapter 8
Interactions

Smart phones, tablets and computers provide calendars, e-mail, access to social media, some forms of instant messaging, SMS and phone calls. Even a computer might place a phone call through the use of a service like Skype. These are all forms of interaction which are covered in this chapter.

8.1   Social messages

Several websites, including Twitter and Facebook in particular, provide the ability to post messages for other people to read. These messages may have associated content, such as a picture or an audio clip. The TouchDevelop API provides facilities for downloading such messages and for posting new messages.

The social resource provides the two methods listed in Table 8-1 for creating a new message and for retrieving messages from a website. A simple example of obtaining messages from the two supported social networks and displaying them might be as follows.

```
var TD msgs := social → search("twitter", "#touchdevelop")
var more msgs := social → search("facebook", "TouchDevelop")
// combine the two collections into one
TD msgs → add many(more msgs)
// reorder and display the messages
TD msgs → sort by date
TD msgs → post to wall
```

Table 8-1: Messaging methods of the social service

Methods	Description
social→create message(message : String) : Message	Creates a new message with the text body provided.
social→search(network : String, terms : String) : Message Collection	Searches twitter or Facebook for recent messages matching the search terms provided.

8.1.1 Working with messages

A Message value will usually have a text component, because that is the simplest form of message. However additional information is usually associated with that message. The TouchDevelop API supports many methods for accessing or setting extra content attached to a message. These are all methods of the Message datatype. The methods for accessing, or getting, content are listed in the first table of section C.25 in Appendix C, those for setting content in the second table, and some additional methods in the third table.

It should be remembered that the extra content of a message is not always present. After retrieving one of these optional values, such as media link, the script should perform the test is invalid to verify that the value was actually available.

The share method of a Message instance allows the message to be transmitted in one of a variety of ways. Whichever choice is provided for the *where* parameter, a dialog box is displayed. The message is not sent until a selection has been picked and/or a button to send the message has been tapped.

8.1.2   Message collections

The Message Collection type is a mutable collection of messages. An empty instance may be created with the following call:

```
var msgs := collections → create message collection
```

This empty collection may then be populated using the standard methods for adding new elements to a collection.

Collections of messages may also be created by the social→search and web→feed methods. The web→feed method accesses an RSS stream or Atom feed on the internet and parses that stream into a sequence of messages. An example script which uses the method is *rmc reader* (/fiol).

The Message Collection type provides several methods which are common to all mutable collection types. However there are two additional methods which are particularly useful for managing a message collection. These are listed in Table 8-2.

Table 8-2: Extra methods of the Message Collection datatype

Message Collection Method	Description
reverse: Nothing	Reverses the order of the messages in the collection
sort by date : Nothing	Sorts the messages by their associated date and time values, from newest to oldest

8.2   Locations, places, maps

Many messages, pictures and media resources have location information associated with them. A location is implemented as a pair of geographical coordinates. However, web services exist for finding a place name near to the location, for pinpointing the location on a map, and for obtaining directions from one location to another.

A location can be created or described by using the methods of the locations resource. These methods are listed in Table 8-3.

In addition to the methods provided by the locations service, location values can be obtained from several other sources. Here is a list of the possibilities.

- senses → current location
- senses → current location accurate
- maps → directions
- location method of the Link datatype
- center method of the Map datatype
- location method of the Message datatype
- location method of the Picture datatype
- location method of the Place datatype

Table 8-3: Methods of the locations service

Method	Description
locations → create location(latitude : Number, longitude : Number) : Location	Creates a new location from its coordinates
locations → create location list : Location Collection	Creates an empty list of locations
locations → describe location(location : Location) : String	Finds a name or an address for a location using Bing
locations → search location(address : String, postal code : String, city : String, country : String) : Location	Looks up the coordinates of an address using Bing

Locations are closely associated with maps. The TouchDevelop API provides both a maps service and a Map datatype. Maps are provided through use of Bing. The methods of the maps service are listed in Table 8-4 and the methods of the Map datatype in Table 8-5.

A small example of using locations and the Bing map service is provided by the script *go to picture* (/gpona). The entire script is reproduced below.

```
action main( )
    // Picks a picture in the library and displays
    // directions to the location where it was taken.
```

```
var pic := media → choose picture
var loc := pic → location
if loc → is invalid then
    wall → prompt("This picture does not have location information.")
else        .
    maps → open directions("", senses → current location, "", loc)
```

The Place datatype provides a wrapper for a location so that additional information can be attached to the location. There are both getter and setter methods for the different kinds of additional information. They are listed in the tables of Section C.37 in Appendix C. In addition to these methods, there the usual is invalid and post to wall methods and two more. They are check in, which is provided for Facebook interactions, and to string which creates a string representation of a place.

Table 8-4: Methods of the maps service

Method	Description
maps→ create full map : Map	Creates a full screen Bing map
maps → create map : Map	Creates a Bing map
maps → directions(from : Location, to : Location, walking : Boolean) : Location Collection	Provides a point by point itinerary to get from the one location to another. If walking is true, the route is suitable for walking; otherwise a vehicle route is assumed
maps → open directions(start search : String, start loc : Location, end search : String, end loc : Location) : Nothing	Opens the Bing map application to show the route from one point to another. The two end points can be specified by either a search term or a location. The search term should be "" if the location is to be used.
maps → open map(center : Location, search : String, zoom : Number) : Nothing	Opens the Bing map application around a central point specified by either a search term or a location; zoom is 0 (close) to 1 (far)

8.3   Emails

A TouchDevelop script can prepare an email message ready for transmission, but it does not actually send it. The following short script prepares a message:

```
var msg := social → create message("The dinner party is tonight!")
```

```
msg → set from("your friendly host")
msg → set to("another@outlook.com")
msg → set title("Invitation reminder")
msg → share("email")
```

When these commands are executed, the last one (the share method call) asks which mail account should be used (if more than one has been set up on the phone) and then invokes the phone's email application. The message is not sent until a *send* button in that application is tapped.

Table 8-5: Methods of the Map datatype

Map Method	Description
add line(locations : Location Collection, color : Color, thickness : Number) : Nothing	Fits a line through the list of locations, drawing the line with the given thickness and color
add link(link : Link, background : Color, foreground : Color) : Nothing	Adds a link pushpin to the map at the location associated with the link value
add message(msg : Message, background : Color, foreground : Color) : Nothing	Adds a message pushpin to the map at the location associated with the message value
add picture(location : Location, picture : Picture, background : Color) : Nothing	Adds a picture pushpin to the map at the location associated with the picture value
add place(place : Place, background : Color, foreground : Color) : Nothing	Adds a place pushpin to the map at the location associated with the place value
add text(location : Location, text : String, background : Color, foreground : Color) : Nothing	Adds a text pushpin to the map at the specified location
center : Location	Gets the map center location
clear : Nothing	Removes all lines, pushpins and regions
fill region(locations : Location Collection, fill : Color, stroke : Color, thickness : Number) : Nothing	Draws the edges around a region whose vertices are specified by the list of locations, and fills the region with a given color.
set center(center : Location) : Nothing	Sets the map's center

Map Method	Description
set zoom(level : Number) : Nothing	Sets the map's zoom level, ranging from 1 (whole earth displayed) to 21 (street level)
view pushpins : Nothing	Changes the zoom and center so that all pushpins are visible; the map must be posted on the wall
zoom : Number	Gets the current zoom level

Although the email application can be invoked to send a message, there is no API support for directly reading email with a TouchDevelop script.

8.4   Phone Calls

A script can prepare for a phone call by setting up the number and transferring control to the phone's software for making the call. This facility is provided by the phone resource in the API. The relevant method calls in the API are listed in Table 8-6.

Table 8-6: Methods for handling phone calls

Method	Description
phone → choose phone number: Link	Opens the phone's contact list so that a phone number can be selected
phone → dial phone number(number : String) : Nothing	Sets up a phone call with the provided number, but does not dial the number
phone → save phone number(phone number : String) : Nothing	Opens the phone's contact list to allow the number to added to an existing entry or to a new entry

Some sample code to set up a phone call, ready for initiating the connection, is as follows:

```
var link := phone → choose phone number
phone → dial phone number( link → address)
```

It is not possible to write a script which answers an incoming phone call or which records an audio clip from a phone call.

8.5   2D barcodes

TouchDevelop provides access to the Microsoft Tag service which generates two-dimensional barcodes for text messages and for URLs. These barcodes are square images which can be printed onto documents or publicity material. Most smart phones, whether a Windows phone or not, possess scanning software which enables a user to focus on the barcode with the phone's camera and automatically display the text or visit the webpage.

The barcode generation methods are provided by the tags resource. Its two methods are listed in Table 8-7.

Table 8-7: Barcode generation methods

Method	Description
tags → tag text(text : String, size : Number, bw : Boolean) : Picture	Generates a barcode for the text (up to 1000 characters); size is the width and height of the picture in inches and must be in the range 0.75 to 5.0; if bw is true, the image is generated in black and white, otherwise color.
tags → tag url(url : String, size : Number, bw : Boolean) : Picture	Generates a barcode which points at the supplied URL; size and bw have the same meanings as above.

This sample code generates and displays a barcode:

```
var pic := tags → tag text("TouchDevelop is cool!", 1.0, false)
pic → post to wall
```

The result of running these two statements is shown in Figure 8-1 on the left. The result when the third argument is changed to true appears on the right. Both versions of the barcode work with scanning software.

Figure 8-1: Examples of 2D barcodes

8.6   SMS messages (WP8 only)

SMS is an abbreviation for *Short Message Service*. It is a text messaging service provided by the phone company. It is normally used for sending a message from one cellphone to another cellphone, though some phone companies may provide additional methods for sending or receiving the messages. The original standard for SMS limited message bodies to be a maximum of 140 bytes. (The *twitter* social networking service has the same limit.) Longer messages are automatically broken up into a sequence of short messages.

The TouchDevelop API allows a script to generate an SMS message ready for transmission but it will not actually send it. The user has to perform one additional action.

A few lines of script to generate an SMS message and prepare it for transmission are as follows:

```
var msg := "Come right now, the pizza has arrived"
var recipient := "202 555 1234"
social → send sms( recipient, msg )
```

If that script is executed, the phone's messaging software is activated and the phone displays the standard dialog for sending a SMS message, as shown in Figure 8-2.

Figure 8-2: Sending an SMS message

8.7   Calendar and appointments (WP8 only)

The Windows phone provides a calendar where each day's schedule, comprised of various meetings or appointments, is recorded.

The phone's calendar may be synchronized with one or more calendars held externally, such as a Windows Outlook calendar or a calendar of events on a social network site.

A TouchDevelop script has read-only access to the phone's calendar and can retrieve all the appointments for a specific range of times. As a small example, the following statements will retrieve and display tomorrow's appointments.

```
var start time := time → tomorrow
var end time := start time → add hours(24)
var appts := social → search appointments(start time, end time)
appts → post to wall
```

Note that social→search appointments is the only mechanism provided for accessing the calendar. Each appointment obtained from the calendar has several associated attributes. They may be accessed by using the methods listed in Table 8-8. (The two methods, invalid and post to wall, are omitted from the table.)

Table 8-8: Methods of the Appointment datatype

Appointment Method	Description
attendees : Contact Collection	Gets the list of attendees for the appointment
details : String	Gets the details (body) of the appointment
end time : DateTime	Gets the end time, if available
is all day event : Boolean	Returns true if the appointment is flagged as being all day
is private : Boolean	Returns true if the calendar entry is flagged as being private
location : String	Returns location associated with the appointment
organizer : Contact	Returns the organizer of the appointment, if available
source : String	Returns the appointment's source, i.e. which calendar or social network site it came from
start time : DateTime	Gets the end time, if available
status : String	Returns the user's status for this appointment (free, tentative, busy or outofoffice)
subject : String	Returns the appointment's subject, if available

8.8   Contacts (WP8 and Android only)

Each contact contains several fields. All fields except for the name are optional. The values of these fields may be retrieved by using the access methods listed in first table given in Section C.7 of Appendix C. The values of nearly all these fields may be changed by using the methods listed in second table of that section.

When some part of the contact's information has been changed, the updated contact may be saved back to the phone's contact list by using the social→save contact method.

Table 8-9: Methods for accessing and creating contacts

Method	Description
social→choose contact : Contact	Allows user to select a contact from the phone's contact list
social→choose email : Link	Allows user to select a contact's email from the phone's contact list

Method	Description
social→create contact(nickname : String) : Contact	Creates a new contact with only the nickname field specified
social→save contact(contact : Contact): Nothing	Saves a new contact in the phone's contact list
social→search contacts(prefix : String) : Contact Collection	Searches for contacts whose names begin with the supplied prefix

Chapter 9
Game Board

TouchDevelop includes a "game board" API for writing simple sprite-based games. The API includes a primitive physics engine to simplify common game loops where objects are moving while they experience gravity and friction. Game board elements can be orchestrated using events based on touch and regular timing intervals.

9.1   Introduction

9.1.1   What is a sprite?

In TouchDevelop, sprites are 2D bitmaps that are drawn directly to the screen. Sprites are commonly used to display information such as health bars, number of lives, or text such as scores. Some games, especially older games, are composed entirely of sprites. TouchDevelop allows creation and use of several types of sprite, such as ellipse, rectangle, text and picture. More details about a sprite's capabilities can be obtained from

http://msdn.microsoft.com/en-us/library/bb203919.aspx

9.1.2   Coordinates and units

Positions in the game board API are based on pixels. The origin of the grid is the top left corner when holding the device upright, the x-axis is horizontal, the y-axis vertical. Sprite positions refer to the center of the sprite, i.e., the halfway point of its width and height before any rotation is applied. The reasoning behind this choice is so that sprites can rotate around their center. Future versions of TouchDevelop may provide more control for offsetting sprites from their position. Speed and acceleration are measured in pixels/second and pixels/second^2.

9.1.3   Game program structure

The code for a typical game has an underlying structure like the following.

```
action main( )
    ⊞board := media → create board(640)
    // ... create sprites, add color and features to the board
    ⊞board → post to wall

event gameloop( )
    // ... move objects around ...
    ⊞board → update on wall
```

The gameloop event is triggered approximately every 50 milliseconds, i.e. about 20 times per second.

9.2   The Board datatype

The media resource three two methods for creating a game board; they are listed in Table 9-1. The maximum height supported by TouchDevelop for a board is 640 pixels. A board created by media→create board is 456 pixels wide; a board created by media→create portrait board is 480 pixels wide. A board remains invisible until it is posted to the wall.

Once posted, updates to the board state and the sprites on the board become visible only when calling board→update on wall.

The methods of the Board datatype concerned with the board's dimensions and general appearance are listed in Table 9-2. The board has a background color and a background picture that can be set separately. The default background color is transparent, and no background picture is provided by default. An additional possibility is to copy the images captured by the device's primary camera and use those images as an ever changing background for the board. Only one of these background possibilities can be active at a time.

Table 9-1: Methods to create a board

Methods	Description
media→create board(height : Number) : Board	Creates a new board with the specified height in pixels
media→create portrait board : Board	Creates a new board that fills the entire screen when displayed and assumes the device is held in portrait mode.
media→create landscape board : Board	Creates a new board that fills the entire screen when displayed and assumes the device is held in landscape mode.

9.2.1   Creating sprites

There are four kinds of sprite that display different kinds of visual content. They can have the shapes of ellipses or rectangles. They can be drawn as solid figures, or they can take the form of a piece of updatable text, or be created from a picture. There is a fifth kind of sprite known as an *anchor sprite*. It is invisible and has a special purpose, which is explained below under the heading 'springs and anchors'. Sprites are associated with particular game boards and are created by methods of the Board type. The methods for creating and accessing sprites are listed in Table 9-3.

Sprites have initial positions centered on the board and no speed or angular rotation. These properties can be set for each sprite using the methods of the Sprite datatype.

In addition to the at method, a **for each** loop can be used to access all the sprites on a board. If board is a variable of type Board, then the loop has the following structure.

```
for each sprite in board where true do
    // access the sprite
```

Table 9-2: Methods of Board datatype: appearance

Board Method	Description
clear background camera : Nothing	Removes any association of the board's background image with the camera
clear background picture : Nothing	Removes any background picture provided for the board
height : Number	Returns the board height in pixels
is landscape board : Boolean	Returns true if the board is designed for viewing in landscape mode
set background(color : Color) : Nothing	Sets the background color for the board
set background camera(camera : Camera) : Nothing	Sets the background for the board to be image captured by the primary camera
set background picture(picture : Picture) : Nothing	Sets a background picture to display on the board
width : Number	Returns the board width in pixels

Table 9-3: Methods of Board datatype: creating / accessing sprites

Board Method	Description
at(i : Number) : Sprite	Returns sprite number i on this board instance (0 ≤ i < count)
count : Number	Returns the number of sprites on this board
create anchor(width : Number, height : Number) : Sprite	Creates an invisible unmovable anchor sprite
create ellipse(width : Number, height : Number) : Sprite	Creates a sprite with an elliptical shape
create picture(picture : Picture) : Sprite	Creates a sprite with the same dimensions and image as the picture
create rectangle(width : Number, height : Number) : Sprite	Creates a sprite with a rectangular shape
create sprite set : Sprite Set	Creates an empty collection of sprites
create text(width : Number, height : Number, fontSize : Number, text : String) : Sprite	Creates a sprite which is displayed on the board as a text string

During games it is very useful to have several collections of sprites. For example, one collection contains spacecraft, another asteroids, and so on.

A sprite collection can be created as an instance of the Sprite Set datatype. The method create sprite set creates a new set which can hold sprites associated with the Board instance. Sprites can be added to and removed from these sets by using methods of the Sprite Set datatype.

9.2.2   Obstacles and boundaries

Obstacles are walls that can be added to the board. Walls cannot be moved once created. Moving sprites which encounter an obstacle will bounce back with a speed determined by the product of the obstacle's *elasticity* and the sprite's elasticity. Elasticities of 1 for both the obstacle and the sprite means the sprite will maintain its full speed, albeit in a different direction. If one or both elasticities are 0, there will be full absorption of the impulse; the sprite will stick to the wall. By default, all elasticities are 1.

By default, the board is open, meaning it has no boundary. Sprites moving off the visual part of the board will simply continue moving away. Since it is common to need reflecting walls around the board, the create boundary(distance) method can be used to create a reflective set of walls around the board at the given distance from the board's edges. The elasticity of these reflective walls is 1, i.e. the sprite's speed is not reduced. If the distance of the boundary from the board's edge is larger than the sprite's size, a sprite can disappear off the screen before bouncing back and re-appearing. If the distance is set as a negative number, the boundaries are located inside the board area.

The methods for creating obstacles and boundaries are listed in Table 9-4.

9.2.3   Forces and animation

Gravity and friction

A uniform force can be applied to all sprites on the board. For instance, there could be a force which pulls all objects towards the bottom of the screen, mimicking the force of *gravity*. However this gravitational force need not remain constant. If the device possesses the necessary sensors, the script can repeatedly use the device's orientation, as determined by its gyroscope, or its accelerometer readings to vary the force and direction of gravity that is experienced by objects in the game.

Table 9-4: Methods of Board datatype: obstacles / boundaries

Board Method	Description
create boundary(distance : Number) : Nothing	Create perfectly reflective walls around the board at the given distance from its edges
create obstacle(x : Number, y : Number, xsegment : Number, ysegment : Number, elasticity : Number) : Nothing	Create a solid obstacle in the form of a line starting at x, y and continuing xsegment, ysegment in the x and y directions; elasticity is in the range 0 (sticky) to 1 (fully reflective)

Once sprites are given speeds or if gravity has been made non-zero, the board engine can update a sprite's position. To update all sprite positions for one time step, the board→evolve method should be invoked. The duration of the time step is simply the time since the last call to board→evolve or since the creation of the board.

A simple script which uses obstacles and gravity appears in Figure 9-1.

Figure 9-1: Example script: a moving ball (/nyuc)

```
action main( )
    ⊞board:= media → create board(640)
    ⊞board → set background(colors → white)
    ⊞board → create boundary(0)
    ⊞board → create obstacle(100,100,50,50,1)
    var ball := ⊞board → create ellipse(20,20)
    ⊞board → post to wall

event gameloop( )
    var p := senses → acceleration quick → scale(1000)
    ⊞board → set gravity(p→x, p→y)
    ⊞board → evolve
    ⊞board → update on wall
```

The script creates a board and adds a reflective wall around the entire board. It then creates a small obstacle wall and a single sprite in the shape of a ball. Within the game loop, the accelerometer is used to set the gravity on the game board. To make the ball move more quickly, the acceleration is scaled by a factor of 1000.

By default, a sprite keeps on moving without slowing down. It can lose speed only if it moves in an opposite direction to gravity or if it loses energy in a collision with an obstacle whose elasticity is less than 1. If it is desirable to make sprites slow down by themselves, a default *friction* setting can be provided for the board or for each sprite individually.

Each sprite can have its own friction setting but, if not set, each sprite experiences the default friction from the board. A friction is defined as the fraction of the forward speed that is experienced as a backwards force. A friction of 0 corresponds to no friction, and a friction of 1 means the sprite will not move at all.

The methods for animating the board and applying forces to sprites are summarized in Table 9-5.

Table 9-5: Methods of Board datatype: forces / animation

Board Method	Description
create spring(sprite1 : Sprite, sprite2 : Sprite, stiffness : Number) : Nothing	Creates an attractive force between two sprites; stiffness determines the strength of the force
evolve : Nothing	Update the positions of all sprites on the board
set friction(friction : Number) : Nothing	Set the default friction for all sprites which do not have their own friction settings; friction is in the range 0 (no loss of speed) to 1 (total loss of speed)
set gravity(x : Number, y : Number) : Nothing	Sets a uniform acceleration vector x,y for all sprites on the board

Springs and anchors

A spring can be added between two sprites to make them accelerate towards each other. A spring is created by the create spring method listed in Table 9-5. The force of the spring is proportional to the distance between the two sprites. The further they are apart, the stronger the force. The constant of proportionality is determined by the stiffness parameter of create spring. The larger its value, the stronger the attractive force.

Without friction to dissipate energy over time, sprites linked by a spring will oscillate indefinitely. With friction, they will eventually converge on the same point. A common scenario is to fix one of the two spring-linked sprites on the board (make it unmovable).

One way to produce an unmovable sprite is to set its friction to 1. An alternative possibility is to use an invisible *anchor sprite*. The create anchor method creates the invisible sprite with its friction set to 1.0. A sprite linked to an anchor via a spring therefore oscillates around the anchor. Giving the sprite an initial velocity vector perpendicular to the direction of the spring causes the sprite to circle around the anchor. With multiple anchors and springs, some interesting oscillation paths can be produced.

9.3   The Sprite datatype

Sprites are movable objects which visually represent parts of a game, such as space ships and asteroids. New sprites are created with methods of the Board datatype. Once a sprite has been created, its position, speed, mass, color, *etc.*, can be set with methods of the Sprite datatype.

Visual attributes

Visual attributes of a sprite such as its color and size are accessed through the methods listed in Table 9-6.

Table 9-6: Methods of Sprite datatype: visual attributes

Board Method	Description
color : Color	Returns the sprite's color
height : Number	Returns the sprite's height in pixels
hide : Nothing	Hide the sprite (make it invisible)
is visible : Boolean	Returns true if the sprite is not hidden
move clip(x : Number, y : Number) : Nothing	Adjusts the clipping region around a sprite created from a picture
opacity : Number	Returns the sprite's opacity; 0 is transparent, 1 is opaque
picture : Picture	Returns the picture for a picture sprite
set clip(left : Number, top : Number, width : Number, height : Number) : Nothing	Sets a clipping region for a sprite created from a picture (an image sprite)
set color(color : Color) : Nothing	Sets the sprite's color (ignored if it is a picture sprite)

Board Method	Description
set height(height : Number) : Nothing	Sets the sprite's height, measured in pixels
set opacity(opacity : Number) : Nothing	Sets the sprite's opacity; 0 is transparent, 1 is opaque
set picture(pic : Picture) : Nothing	Replaces the picture for sprite created from a picture (ignored for non-picture sprites)
set text(text : String) : Nothing	Replaces the text for a sprite created from a text string (ignored for non-text sprites)
set width(width : Number) : Nothing	Sets the sprite's width, measured in pixels
set z index(zindex : Number) : Nothing	Sets the z-index of the sprite
show : Nothing	Show the sprite (the opposite of hide)
text : String	Gets the text from a text sprite
width : Number	Gets the sprite's width, measured in pixels
z index : Number	Gets the z-index of the sprite

The z-index, accessed by the methods set z index and z index, provide control over the order in which sprites are rendered on the screen. If two sprites overlap, the sprite which is rendered second will appear to be on top of the first sprite.

The rendering order can be controlled by the z-index values. When these values are provided, the sprites are rendered in order of their z-indexes, from smallest to largest.

Position and motion

A sprite has a current position and a current angular orientation. Both of these change at rates determined by the sprite's speed and its angular velocity. These attributes of a sprite are accessed or changed by using the methods listed in Table 9-8.

Accelerations, forces and bounces

In the absence of gravity, springs and friction, a sprite will keep moving across the board at a constant velocity until it hits a barrier of some kind. However, in the presence of these effects, the sprite's velocity does change.

Springs are created using the create spring method of the board. They have been covered already. The acceleration induced on a sprite by a spring's force is inversely proportional to the sprite's mass.

Table 9-7: Methods of Sprite datatype: position / velocity

Board Method	Description
angle : Number	Gets the sprite's angle in degrees
angular speed : Number	Gets the angular velocity in degrees/sec
move(deltax : Number, deltay : Number) : Nothing	Adjusts the sprite's position by deltax and deltay in the x,y dimensions
move towards(other : Sprite, fraction : Number) : Nothing	Moves this sprite towards other sprite by specified fraction of the distance
set angle(angle: Number) : Nothing	Sets the angle of the sprite in degrees
set angular speed(speed : Number) : Nothing	Sets angular velocity in degrees/sec
set pos(x : Number, y : Number) : Nothing	Sets the position of the sprite to new x and y coordinates
set speed(vx : Number, vy : Number) : Nothing	Sets the x and y speed components of the sprite, vx and vy are in pixels/sec
set speed x(vx : Number) : Nothing	Sets just the x component of the speed, in pixels/sec
set speed y(vy : Number) : Nothing	Sets just the y component of the speed, in pixels/sec
set x(x : Number) : Nothing	Sets the x coordinate of the sprite
set y(y : Number) : Nothing	Sets the y coordinate of the sprite
speed towards(other : Sprite, magnitude : Number) : Nothing	Sets the speed of this sprite to move towards another sprite; the speed is in pixels/sec
speed x : Number	Gets the x component of the sprite's speed in pixels/sec
speed y : Number	Gets the y component of the sprite's speed in pixels/sec
x : Number	Gets the x coordinate of the position
y : Number	Gets the y coordinate of the position

The heavier the sprite, the longer it will take for a spring to have its full effect. Each sprite has a default mass which is simply the product of the sprite's width and height. However, that default can be overridden by the sprite's set mass method. A mass cannot be made zero or negative.

A gravitational force can be specified for the board and this applies a force to every sprite, excluding any anchor sprites. The size of the force is proportional to the sprite's mass. However, the effect of the force on a sprite's speed is inversely proportional to the mass, so the acceleration induced by gravity is independent of the sprite's mass.

An additional force which works to slow down a moving sprite is *friction*. A friction value can be specified for the board using its set friction method. This becomes the default friction value for all sprites on the board. However, friction can also be set for individual sprites using the set friction method of the Sprite instance.

All these forces listed above combine to produce the net force on a sprite and cause a sprite to move. If the combined forces do not produce the desired effect, there is one more adjustment which can be made. This adjustment is produced by the set acceleration method, covered in the next subsection of this chapter.

When a sprite hits an obstacle, the sprite rebounds with a new velocity in a new direction. The magnitude of that new velocity is determined by the product of the elasticities of the sprite and the obstacle. If both elasticities are 1, it is a perfect bounce which loses no energy. The sprite loses no speed. If the product is 0, the sprite stops and stays stuck to the obstacle.

The current implementation of the game board does not detect collisions between sprites. It requires too much computation, especially if there are many sprites. One sprite will simply appear to pass through another sprite.

The methods for accessing friction, mass and elasticity settings for a sprite are listed in Table 9-8.

9.3.1   *Managing sprites*

Implementing a game will usually require some extra programming which is not provided by the features of boards and sprites covered so far. If for example, the game requires forces of a different nature than those provided by springs and gravity, or if collisions between sprites need to be handled, then the additional Sprite methods listed in Table 9-9 should be useful.

Table 9-8: Methods of Sprite datatype: mass, friction, elasticity

Board Method	Description
elasticity : Number	Get the sprite's elasticity as a fraction of speed preservation per bounce (0 to 1)
friction : Number	Get the sprite's friction measured as a fraction of speed loss (0 to 1)
mass : Number	Get the sprite's mass
set elasticity(elasticity : Number) : Nothing	Set the sprite's elasticity as a fraction of speed preservation per bounce (0 to 1)
set friction(friction : Number) : Nothing	Set the sprite's friction measured as a fraction of speed loss (0 to 1)
set mass(mass : Number) : Nothing	Set the sprite's mass (a value greater than zero)

Table 9-9: Methods of Sprite datatype: additional features

Sprite Method	Description
acceleration x : Number	Get the x component of the sprite's current acceleration in pixels/sec2
acceleration y : Number	Get the y component of the sprite's current acceleration in pixels/sec2
delete : Nothing	Delete the sprite
equals(other : Sprite) : Boolean	Returns true if this sprite is the same sprite as the other one
location : Location	Gets the sprite's geo location (as assigned by the set location method)
overlap with(sprites : Sprite Set) : Sprite Set	Returns the subset of sprites which overlap with this sprite
overlaps with(other : Sprite) : Boolean	Returns true if the two sprites overlap
set acceleration(vx : Number, vy : Number) : Nothing	Set the sprite's acceleration in pixels/sec2
set acceleration x(vx : Number) : Nothing	Set the x component of the sprite's acceleration in pixels/sec2
set acceleration y(vy : Number) : Nothing	Set the x component of the sprite's acceleration in pixels/sec2
set location(location : Location) : Nothing	Sets the sprite's geo location

For collision detection, the overlap with and overlaps with methods should help. Provided that the sprites are not moving so fast or the sprites are not so small that one sprite completely passes through another sprite during one time step, the colliding sprites will overlap when drawn on the board. The two methods allow the collision to be detected, and then the directions of motion of the two sprites can be overridden to simulate the two sprites bouncing off each other.

If, for example, the sprites represent planets revolving around a star, a spring force between a planet and the star is a long way from being a proper implementation of gravitational attraction. In this situation, a good approach would be to avoid using springs altogether and to calculate the force induced on a planet by gravitational attraction. Combining that force with the planet's current velocity and its mass allows the acceleration induced by gravitational attraction to be calculated. And that acceleration can be explicitly given to the planet by the set acceleration method. When an acceleration is specified, the effect of the acceleration is in addition to any accelerations induced by springs and gravity. The acceleration value remains in effect until changed by a new call to set acceleration.

Another possibility is that a sprite needs to be destroyed and removed from the board. In this case, the delete method should be invoked. The sprite instance is automatically removed from the board and from all sprite collections. Any references to the instance become invalid.

9.4   The Sprite Collection datatype

When writing simple games with multiple objects of the same kind (e.g. multiple shots, missiles, *etc.*), it quickly becomes necessary to group related sprites into collections. The Board datatype provides the method board→create sprite set which creates a new empty collection of sprites.

Sprite Set provides most of the methods common to the mutable collection types. These are the methods add, add many, at, count, is invalid, and post to wall. They were covered in Chapter 2. However, there is a major difference. All the other collection types are lists of values. It implies that the same value can appear in the list several times. A Sprite Set is, in contrast, an *ordered set.* A value can appear at most once in the set. The elements of the set are ordered by their index positions.

In addition to the standard methods listed above, the Sprite Set datatype has the special methods listed in Table 9-10. Note that the add method appears in the table even though it is a standard method for mutable collections. This is because the Sprite Set version of the add method is slightly different. It only adds an element if it would be a new element, and it returns a Boolean result to indicate whether an element was actually added.

Table 9-10: Additional or modified Sprite Set methods

Sprite Method	Description
add(sprite : Sprite) : Boolean	Adds sprite to set if not already present; the result is true if it was not present already.
add from(old set : Sprite Set, sprite : Sprite) : Boolean	Adds the sprite to the new set and removes it from the old set; the result is true if the sprite was in the old set.
contains(sprite : Sprite) : Boolean	Returns true if the sprite is in the set
index of(sprite : Sprite) : Number	Returns the index of the sprite in the set; the result is -1 if not in the set
remove first : Sprite	Removes the sprite which was added to the set before all the others

9.5   Touching and board events

The board has six specific kinds of events which are covered in the subsections below. All but one of these events are triggered when the user touches the screen and taps, swipes or drags a finger across the board.

9.5.1   Board touching actions

In addition to events, the Board datatype provides five methods which provide information about how the screen has been touched. These methods are listed in Table 9-11. However the tap, swipe and drag events explained later in this section are easier to program and their use is recommended.

Table 9-11: Touch methods of the Board datatype

Sprite Method	Description
touch current : Vector3	Returns the coordinates of the current touch point on the board; the z component is 0.
touch end : Vector3	Returns the coordinates of the last touch point on the board; the z component is 0
touch start : Vector3	Returns the coordinates of the latest start point for a touch gesture on the board; the z component is 0
touch velocity : Vector3	Returns the final swiping velocity after a touch has gesture; the z component is 0
touched : Boolean	Returns true if the board has been touched

9.5.2   gameloop event

The gameloop event contains code that needs to be run regularly and frequently. The event is triggered about every 50ms. It is a natural location to contain collision detection code, or to monitor the passage of time.

The gameloop event code should be efficient. If it takes too long to execute, the display may stutter and collisions may go undetected.

9.5.3   tap board event

The tap board event fires if there is tap anywhere on the board except on a position where a sprite is located. Tapping means that one's finger leaves the screen at approximately the same position as where it first touched. Otherwise, the software will report a swipe event instead. The event fires once the finger is lifted.

As an example, the code below creates a new ball wherever there is a tap the board.

```
event tap board: board(x,y)
    var sprite := ⊞board → create ellipse(10,10)
    sprite → set pos(x,y)
```

The tap board event has two parameters x and y which give the position where the tap occurred.

9.5.4   swipe board event

The swipe board event is similar, except that the event code is passed four parameters. The first two show where the swipe started and the second two show the extent of the swipe in the x and y dimensions.

As an example, the code below creates a new sprite and gives it an initial speed which corresponds to the extent of the swipe.

```
event swipe board: board(x, y, delta x, delta y)
    var sprite := ▣board → create ellipse(10,10)
    sprite → set pos(x,y)
    sprite → set speed(delta x, delta y)
```

9.5.5   tap sprite in XXX event

Tap events can be provided for sprites held in different sprite collections. This makes it easier to program one kind of action for a spaceship, say, and a different kind of action when tapping an asteroid, say.

If, for example, there is a global data variable named spaceships with the type Sprite Set, then an event named tap sprite in asteroids can be provided. The event is passed four parameters. These are the sprite which was tapped, the index of the sprite in the sprite set, and the coordinates of the sprite on the board.

A sample of code which uses the event is as follows:

```
action main( )
    ...
    ▣asteroids := ▣board → create sprite set
    // populate the board with spaceships and asteroids
    ...

event tap sprite in asteroids(sprite, index, x, y)
    // change the asteroid's color
    sprite → set color(colors → red)
```

9.5.6   swipe sprite in XXX event

The swipe sprite event is similar to the tap sprite event, except that one's finger is swiped across the screen and the extent of the swipe is passed as two additional parameters. For example, the following code will cause the sprite which is swiped to start moving in the direction of the swipe.

```
event swipe sprite in asteroids(sprite, index, x, y, delta x, delta y)
    sprite → set speed(delta x, delta y)
```

9.5.7   drag sprite in XXX event

A *drag event* does not wait for the finger to be lifted from the screen, as with the tap and swipe events. It fires while one's finger is still on the screen. It will repeatedly fire while the finger is in motion across the screen. The event is passed very similar parameters to the swipe sprite event, except that the last two parameters provide the extent of the dragging motion (so far).

The event can be used to temporarily set the speed of a dragged sprite to 0 and to display it at the current drag position. In this way, it will appear that the sprite is being held at the finger's position.

Here is example coding with the asteroids:

```
event drag sprite in asteroids(sprite, index, x, y, delta x, delta y)
    sprite → set speed(0, 0)
    sprite → set pos(x, y)
```

When the finger is lifted at the end of the motion, a swipe sprite event is triggered (if event code for that action has been provided).

9.5.8   tap sprite SSS, swipe sprite SSS, drag sprite SSS

Instead of having events associated with sprite sets, it is possible to have events associated with an individual sprite. To do this, the sprite must be promoted to be a global data variable (in the data section of a script).

If the data variable is named SSS, then the corresponding event names are tap sprite SSS, swipe sprite SSS and drag sprite SSS.

9.6   Debugging games

To make it a bit simpler to debug sprite position and speed related problems
in scripts, the debug mode for the board can be enabled.

⊡board→set debug mode(true)

If debug mode is on, the board will display the position and speed of a sprite
next to the sprite content. Additionally, the width and height is displayed as
a box around the sprite. Also, in debug mode, even invisible sprites are
displayed. This can be useful for finding forgotten sprites or where anchors
are placed.

Chapter 10
UI with Boxes and Pages

A well-designed user interface that takes full advantage of the screen is essential for giving a professional look and feel to a program. The *page* and *boxed* constructs in TouchDevelop provide a powerful means of laying out information on the screen. A unique feature to assist script developers is that a running script can be suspended while the format of information currently displayed on the screen is changed, and then the script's execution can be resumed.

10.1 Page Overview

A page is invoked in a similar manner to an action. However, when it is invoked, it takes over the whole screen. Everything displayed on the screen is created by the code belonging to that screen (or by actions invoked by the page).

Pages are managed in a stack-like manner. When the code in page A causes page B to be displayed, B takes over the screen. However, when B is finished or when the user taps the back button, the screen reverts to show what had been displayed by A just before B. Similarly, page B could have caused page C to be displayed, and when C is finished, the screen returns to show page B again.

The code for a page is divided into two main parts: an *initialize* section and a *display* section. When the page is invoked, the screen is cleared to be blank and then the code in the initialize section is executed. This code can execute all kinds of statements in the scripting language except that *it cannot display anything on the screen*. If it attempts to change anything on this blank screen, the script stops execution with an error report. The purpose of the initialize section is to initialize global variables, especially global variables which will be used in the display section of the page.

The display section of a page is responsible for rendering the images and text on the screen. The box construct, explained below, is used to manage the placement of information on the screen. There is a major restriction on what the code in the display section is allowed to do. *The display section cannot make assignments to any global variables*. If the code in the display section attempts to execute such an assignment, or calls an action which attempts such an assignment, the script stops execution with an error report.

The restrictions on the contents of the initialize section and display section impose a certain style of programming on the script developer. However these restrictions also provide a significant benefit. They permit the script's developer to modify the layout and contents of the screen while the script execution is suspended and then resume execution with the new screen layout in effect. A developer can therefore correct and/or improve the script's user interface without having to stop and restart the script from the beginning.

10.2   Box Overview

The display section of a page is responsible for rendering visual elements on the screen. Within that screen area, any value which can be displayed on the wall can be displayed here too.

There is, however, a special feature available for use only within the display section of a page. The new feature is called a *box*, and it is introduced in a script with the keyword **boxed**. Any collection of graphical elements can be boxed, which means that the collection can be treated as a single unit known as a box. That box becomes a graphical element in its own right.

A box represents a rectangular region of the screen. The size of the rectangle will normally default to whatever is needed to enclose its contents. Alternatively, either or both dimensions can be specified or constrained to be within desired ranges. Scroll bars can be added to a box if desired.

An important part of a graphical user interface is the ability to input information. Code can be attached to a box which is executed when the box is tapped (or clicked with a mouse). A box containing text can be marked as editable, and code can be attached to that box which is executed whenever the text contents are changed. The attached code must take the form of a *change handler*. For a click event, the change handler is a parameterless action. For the action of changing text, it is an action which takes a single String parameter; that string is a copy of the new text.

10.3   Examples of Boxes and Pages

A page can be displayed either by making it into the first action executed when the script is started, or by using a **push** statement. The first of these choices is automatic if you select the script template named *pages* when starting to create the script. The first example discussed here was created in this way.

10.3.1 Page Example 1 (/bvhugenw)

Figure 10.1 is very similar to the *scripts* template. However some changes have been made to illustrate a couple of important points.

The **boxed** keyword creates a new box. It is a *container box*, because it is intended to hold graphical elements drawn on the screen. The contents and the formatting of that box are specified by the indented code underneath. In this example, two lines of text are written to the wall, which means that they are written as the contents of the box. After the script is run, the screen has the contents shown in Figure 10.2(a).

The lines of text are written one below the other and are left-justified within the box. A vertical layout of graphical elements with left justification is the default. Both of these defaults can be overridden.

Figure 10.1: Page Example 1 (/bvhugenw)

```
page main ( )
initialize
    // do nothing
display
    box → set background(colors → from rgb(1 ,0.75, 0.75))
    boxed
        box → set font size(1)
        box → set foreground(colors → red)
        box → set background(colors → yellow)
        box → set margins(2, 2, 2, 2)
        "Hello world!" → post to wall
        box → set font size(3)
        box → set foreground(colors → green)
        "Hello world once more!" → post to wall
        box → set foreground(colors → blue)
```

The surprise of the example is that the sizes and colors of the two lines of text are exactly the same. The reason is that the graphical elements defined inside the box, which are the two textual strings in this example, are not rendered until all the statements inside the box have been executed. It is only the last change to the foreground color and the last change to the font size which has any effect.

The two lines of text are themselves boxes, but they are known as *leaf boxes* because they do not contain any boxes at a lower level. It is possible to see the extents of all the boxes on the screen by tapping the pause button in the top right-hand corner of the screen. Figure 10.2(b) shows the browser window after pausing the script. Thin blue lines surround the two lines of text separately. The two leaf boxes taken together comprise the entire contents of the container box, and correspond to the code inside the **boxed** construct. That is why the background color of box boxes is yellow. The pink region surrounding the container box corresponds to the entire page – it is the frame within which the boxes have been drawn. The statement box → set margins(2, 2, 2, 2) affects the placement of the container box inside that enclosing frame.

As the code of Page Example 1 shows, it is possible to specify some kinds of formatting for the frame by using the box variable immediately inside the display section of the code.

Leaf boxes are created in various ways which include posting text on the wall, or posting images from the art section of the script onto the wall. The formatting of text in a leaf box is inherited from its enclosing container box.

Figure 10.2: (a) Result from Page Example 1

(b) Paused Result of Page Example 1

10.3.2 Page Example 2 (/hnimxaiw)

The second example introduces events which are executed when a box is clicked and demonstrates the need for the initialize section in a page (Figure 10.3).

The display section of the page defines three boxes. Because the display section makes the method call box → use horizontal layout, the three boxes are drawn from left to right across the screen. Furthermore, the boxes are vertically aligned so that their middle points are in a straight line.

The first box contains text copied from the global variable s, and draws it with a font whose size is specified by the global variable, size. The code also sets attributes of the box so that the text will wrap onto multiple lines if it does not fit, and solid lines are drawn around the box.

The second and third boxes are both intended to be clickable. They are drawn to have the same size and use the same colors. Therefore, rather than duplicating the code for the two boxes, the code to set each box's attributes has been defined inside the action named create button. Whenever the identifier box is used inside that action, it refers to the current box which is being defined.

After calling the create button action for each box, the on tapped method is invoked to attach a change handler to the box. For a tapping action, the change handler takes the form of an action with no parameters, and that action has to be defined at this point in the script using a **where** clause.

The code inside a change handler can do anything allowed in a TouchDevelop script except assign values to local variables, change any attributes of the current box or directly change what is being displayed. *If the action of tapping the box is to have any effect on the current page, the change handler must communicate the changes via global variables.*

The change handler for the box which displays the text "Click Here" increments a global variable named cnt and then uses the new value of cnt to construct a string value stored in the global variable s. It should be noted that s was used to provide the contents displayed inside the first box drawn on the page.

Along similar lines, the change handler for the box which displays the text "Make Larger" increments a global variable which specifies the font size used for text displayed in the first box on the page.

When the script is run, the first box is initially empty. However, when the "Click Here" box is tapped, the first box changes to display the string "It was clicked 1 times". Each subsequent tapping action changes that 1 to 2, then to 3 and so on. The change to the box contents on the screen occurs because the entire page is redrawn any time something happens which may affect the page. The reasons for redrawing the page include:

- executing a change handler on the page,
- clicking the suspend button at the top right of the screen and then resuming the script,
- displaying another page and then returning to this page,
- any global variables or records have been modified.

Figure 10.3: Page Example 2 (/hnimxaiw)

```
page main ()
initialize
    ⊞ s := " "
    ⊞ cnt := 0
    ⊞ size := 1
display
    box → use horizontal layout
    box → set vertical align("center")
    boxed
        box → set width(30)
        box → set font size(⊞ size)
        box → set text wrapping(true, 15)
        box → set margins(1, 2, 1, 2)
        box → set border(colors→black,0.1)
        ⊞ s → post to wall
    boxed
        ▷ create button("Click Here")
        box → on tapped(handler)
            where handler( ) is
                ⊞ cnt := ⊞ cnt + 1
                ⊞ s := "It was clicked "
                    || ⊞ cnt || " times"
    boxed
        ▷ create button("Make Larger")
        box → on tapped(handler)
            where handler( ) is
                ⊞ size := ⊞ size + 1
```

```
private action create button (
    text : String)
do
    box → set background(
        colors → yellow)
    box → set width range(5, 15)
    box → set height range(0, 5)
    box → set border(
        colors → black, 0.1)
    box → set vertical align(
        "center")
    box → set horizontal align(
        "center")
    box → set margins(1, 1, 1, 1)
    box → set padding(1, 1, 1, 1)
    text → post to wall

data cnt : Number
data s : String
data size : Number
```

The screen after tapping the "Click Here" and "Make Larger" buttons a few times each is shown in Figure 10.4. Note that the *text wrapping* attribute of the first box was set, and when the font size was increased, the string wrapped onto two lines of text. No height was specified for the box, so it simply grows taller to accommodate the two lines of text.

Figure 10.4: Result of Running Page Example 2

10.3.3   Page Example 3 (/wrsonnwh)

The third example script shows the use of a change handler to process editable text and the nesting of boxes to achieve a desired layout for the graphical elements.

The script shown in Figure 10.5 allows the user to enter English language text into the left-hand box. Every time the user pauses, the change handler is invoked. Its input parameter is a copy of the current version of the text. That input parameter is normally assigned, unchanged, to the global variable associated with this box. (The editor ensures that there is always such a variable and it will have the String type.) However additional actions can be added to the change handler. In this example, that additional action is to invoke the Bing language translation service and translate the English language input into French, The French version of the text is displayed in the right-hand box.

A snapshot of the screen after the script has been used to translate one sentence is shown in

A production version of this script might allow the user to select both the source language and the destination language for the translation. This nicer version of the script would presumably use the full names of the languages rather than two letter abbreviations. It would likely also perform the translation only when the user clicks on the arrow between the two boxes. It can be disconcerting to have partial translations popping up and changing as one is typing text into the left-hand box. Also, an internet connection is made every time the text is translated and this can be undesirable for a tablet device communicating via a cellphone connection. These enhancements are left as an exercise for the reader.

Figure 10.6.

Figure 10.5: Page Example 3 (/wrsonnwh)

```
page main ()
initialize
    ⊞ src lang := "en"
    ⊞ dest lang := "fr"
    ⊞ src text := " "
    ⊞ dest text := " "
display
    box → set horizontal align("center")
    boxed
        box → set font size(2)
        box → set foreground(
            colors → red)
        ("Live translation from " ∥
            ⊞ src lang ∥ " to " ∥
            ⊞ dest lang) → post to wall
    boxed
        box → use horizontal layout
        box → set vertical align("center")
        boxed
            ▷ create text box
            box → edit("textarea",
            ⊞ src text, handler)
            where handler(
                    text : String) is
                ⊞ src text := text
                ⊞ dest text :=
        languages → translate(⊞ src lang,
        ⊞ dest lang, ⊞ src text)
            boxed
                ✿ Right Arrow → post to wall
            boxed
                ▷ create text box
                ⊞ dest text → post to wall
```

```
private action create text box ()
    box → use horizontal layout
    box → set width(20)
    box → set height(15)
    box → set font size(1.5)
    box → set text wrapping(true, 5)
    box → set border(colors → black,
        0.1)
    box → set padding(5, 2, 2, 2)

data dest lang : String
data dest text : String
data src lang : String
data src text : String

art Right Arrow : Picture
with url:
    "https://az31353.vo.msecnd.net/
    pub/twibazkg"
```

A production version of this script might allow the user to select both the source language and the destination language for the translation. This nicer version of the script would presumably use the full names of the languages rather than two letter abbreviations. It would likely also perform the translation only when the user clicks on the arrow between the two boxes. It can be disconcerting to have partial translations popping up and changing as one is typing text into the left-hand box. Also, an internet connection is made every time the text is translated and this can be undesirable for a tablet device communicating via a cellphone connection. These enhancements are left as an exercise for the reader.

Figure 10.6: Translation produced by Page Example 3

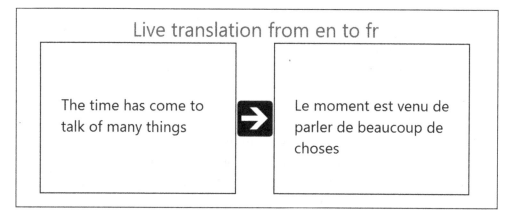

10.4   Working with Pages

The display section of a page works with the entire window of the browser running the script. This window is effectively the current box for any code executed immediately inside the display section; that is, code which is not nested inside a **boxed** construct.

10.4.1   Entering and Leaving a Page

A page is simply a special kind of action. It can be invoked as an entry point of the script if it is public and does not have any parameters. It can also be invoked as though it were an action. If, for example, the script defines a page named show then the page can be displayed by executing the call ▷ show. When code for the script is displayed on the screen, the call statement appears as push ▷ show to indicate that the TouchDevelop run-time is maintaining a stack of pages.

A page which is not used as the entry point of a script can accept input parameters. It cannot have any output parameters.

A page can be exited (terminated) by clicking the back arrow which appears in the top left corner of the webpage. On a Windows phone, the back button achieves the same effect. The page can also be exited by executing the statement wall → pop page. This statement would normally be used inside a change handler. An example appears below.

```
boxed
    "Click here when done" → post to wall
    box → on tapped(handler)
      where  handler( ) is
        wall → pop page
```

10.4.2 Coding Restrictions

The initialization section of a page cannot draw any items on the page. It can declare and use local variables but these variables are not accessible from inside the display section of the page. (They are out of scope.) Normally, the initialization section is used to initialize global variables used in the display section.

The display section of a page can use but not assign to global variables. (Even though change handlers are defined within the display section, they are not considered to be part of the display section.) The display section can use local variables as normal. It can use normal control structures such as loops and if-statements. Its main purpose is to render graphical elements on the current page.

Change handlers attached to boxes on the current page can use and assign to global variables. They can use but they cannot assign to local variables in the display section of the page, provided that they are visible. (Normal scope rules apply.) They cannot draw any items on the screen nor can they set any attributes of the current box.

All the statements in the display section of the page are re-executed and the entire page is re-drawn after control returns from a change handler or when the page becomes the current page again after another page exits or when a global variable or record is changed. In contrast, the code in the initialization section is only executed when a new instance of the page is created and pushed onto the stack of pages.

The identifier box refers to the current box and can be used in any context where there is an active current box. If box is referenced inside an action, then there may or may not be a current box depending on how control reached that action. A run-time error occurs if there is no current box. There is always a current box if control is inside the display section of a page or inside an action called from a page or inside a change handler attached to a box. There is no current box when the initialization section of a page is being executed.

Even though there may be a current box, access may be limited to read only (such as obtaining the current value of box→pixels per em). Invoking a method which sets attributes of the current box is permitted only within the display section of a page or within an action invoked from the display section.

10.5   Live Editing of the User Interface

Pages are easy to debug and modify while a script is executing. There is no need to stop the script and re-start it from the beginning each time that the script developer makes a small change. When the script is running in a browser, a pause button is displayed in the top right corner of the browser's window. The pause button is shown in Figure 10.7.

Figure 10.7: Icons for User Interface Editing

⏸	✏ edit	▶
Suspend	Edit	Resume

Tapping that button causes a very thin blue line to be drawn around each box which is currently displayed on the screen, and the pause button is replaced with a resume button, also shown in Figure 10.7.

The script is no longer running at this point. Clicking inside one of the rectangles composed of thin blue lines causes the rectangle to be augmented with a thicker dotted red rectangle, and causes a button labeled as 'edit' to appear on the screen. The edit button is shown in Figure 10.7. That dotted red rectangle indicates which box has been selected. Double clicking causes an outer enclosing box to be selected instead. Triple clicking, etc., works similarly when the boxed constructs are nested sufficiently deeply.

Clicking the edit button causes the script editor to be invoked on exactly the code for the selected box. On a display monitor which is wide enough, the browser's window is split so that the left-hand side contains the currently displayed page and the right-hand side shows the code for the selected box. (If the view of the page takes up too much screen real estate, it can be removed by clicking the dismiss button in its top left corner.)

The code for the script can now be edited. Changes can be small or they can be major. There is no restriction on which code in the entire script can be changed. When the changes are complete and it is time to see if they had the desired effect, the view of the current page should be dismissed (if that has not been done already) and the resume button, which is now on the left-hand side of the screen, can be tapped.

Resuming the script causes the display section of the current page to be re-executed and the page is re-drawn, reflecting any changes made to the code. The run-suspend-edit-resume cycle can be repeated as many times as desired until the user interface is perfect.

It should be noted that if major changes to the code are made, such as changes to actions called from other places in the script, then the script may need to be restarted from the beginning to see their full effect.

10.6   API Support for Boxes and Pages

The box identifier names a service which has the Box datatype. There is only one instance of this type, it is a *singleton*.

The **boxed** and **page** constructs in TouchDevelop are recent additions to the scripting language and are still being developed. Table 10-1, Table 10-2 and Table 10-3 list the methods provided for the box service at the time of writing. However additional methods may be provided and/or some of the current methods may be modified to work differently. The most reliable and up-to-date source of information about these constructs is the TouchDevelop website.

Table 10-1: General Methods of box Service

Method	Description
set background(c : Color)	Sets the background color
set foreground(c : Color)	Sets the color of items drawn in the box
set height(h : Number)	Sets an exact height for the box
set height range(min : Number, max : Number)	Sets a range of heights for the box
set width(w : Number)	Sets an exact width for the box
set width range(min : Number, max : Number)	Sets a range of widths for the box
set border(c : Color, w : Number)	Sets the color and width of a line drawn around the edge of the box
set horizontal stretch(f: Number)	Controls how box width is computed: f = 0.0 means shrink to fit content, f = 1.0 means expand to fill the frame, f = 0.5 means expand to 50% of frame's width.
set padding(t: Number, r: Number, b: Number, l: Number)	Specify how much space to leave around the box: t, r, b and l determine the top, right, bottom and left sides respectively.
on tapped(handler: Action)	Associates a handler action with the box, and is invoked when the box is tapped

Table 10-2: Text Handling Methods of box Service

Method	Description
set font size(n : Number)	Sets the font size for text displayed in the box; 1.0 is the current default size.
set text wrapping(wrap: Boolean, min: Number)	Specifies whether long text lines should be broken, and what length is too short to be split
set horizontal align(s: String)	Specifies how to format text in the box; the argument is one of "left", "right", "center" or "justify"
pixels per em	Returns the width of the letter 'm' in pixels
edit(style: String, v: String, changehandler: Action)	Displays text from the global variable v which can be edited. The style parameter is one of "textline" "textarea" "number" or "password". The changehandler is invoked each time the text is changed.

Table 10-3: Layout Methods of box Service

Method	Description
use horizontal layout	Arranges boxes and other items from left to right horizontally
use vertical layout	Arranges boxes and other items from top to bottom vertically
use overlay layout	Arrange boxes and other displayed items inside this box as layers drawn on top of each other
set horizontal align(s: String)	s is one of "left" "right" "center" and "justify" to indicate how text and other items in the box are arranged
set vertical align(s: String)	s is one of "top" "bottom" "center" and "baseline" (for text) to indicate how text and other items in the box are arranged vertically

Chapter 11
Authenticating Web Services

There are many web services on the internet which allow client applications to query and store all kinds of structured information. Some web services require the user to authenticate in order to use protected resources.

11.1   Registering your app

A common source of web service calls is to Facebook's Graph API[1]. With this API, you can query and submit pictures, status updates, comments, and more. All interactions are done on behalf of a particular Facebook user. The user has to give permission to the application to access any part of the user's information.

OAuth v2.0 is a common authentication mechanism for web services supported by Microsoft, Facebook, Google, and other companies. TouchDevelop supports the OAuth 2.0 *Implicit Grant* flow protocol as defined in section 4.2 of the specification (http://tools.ietf.org/html/rfc6749). Other protocols are not currently supported. After having negotiated an access token for a protected web services, TouchDevelop offers the ability

---

[1] http://developers.facebook.com/docs/reference/api/

to process and create structured data in formats such as JSON and XML.

Before you can use the OAuth mechanism to access a web service, you need to register the app you are working on with the provider of the web service. Every web service has its own registration mechanism; you must find and follow the instructions provided by the service you want to use.

Somewhere during the registration process you will be asked for a "redirect URI". You MUST enter the following redirect URI precisely.

> https://www.touchdevelop.com/[userid]/oauth

where [userid] is your TouchDevelop user id. This is a short letter combination such as pboj which happens to be the userid for the TouchDevelop Samples user. Point your browser at https://www.touchdevelop.com/me to find out your user id. You will be redirected to a new URL, possibly after being asked to log in. The new URL has the form https://www.touchdevelop.com/[userid].

Only TouchDevelop scripts published under your account will be able to use this redirect URI. See the later section on unique redirect URIs for instructions on how to handle the situation where the OAuth provider you want to use requires unique URIs for each application.

11.2 Authenticating

The OAuth 2.0 authentication is handled through the web→oauth v2 action. The action takes the OAuth URL including the client_id and optional scope or other arguments. Do NOT include the state and redirect_uri arguments; they are automatically added by TouchDevelop.

```
var oauth res := web → oauth v2(url)
```

The response contains the access token or the details about the error, if any. You can then use the access token to sign each request as specified by the service.

```
var access token := oauth res → access token
var call := "http://....?access_token=" ‖ web → url encode(access token)
```

You can use the is expiring action to easily test if an access token is missing or (almost expired).

```
if oauth res → is expiring(100) then
    // Oops, better ask for a new token.
else do nothing
```

Table 11-1: General methods related to OAuth 2.0

Method	Description
web → oauth v2(oauth url : String) : OAuth Response	Authenticate with OAuth 2.0 and receive the access token or error.

Table 11-2: Properties of the OAuth Response type

Method	Description
access token : String	The access token issued by the authorization server.
error : String	A single ASCII [USASCII] error code.
error description : String	(Optional) A human readable error code.
error uri : String	(Optional) A URI identifying a human-readable web page with information about the error, used to provide the client developer with additional information about the error.
expires in : Number	(Optional) The lifetime in seconds of the access token.
is error : Boolean	Indicates if this response is an error.
is expiring(lookup : Number) : Boolean	(Optional) Indicates if the token might expire within the next seconds.
is invalid : Boolean	Returns true if the current instance is useless
others : String Map	(Optional) Additional key-value pairs not covered by the OAuth 2.0 specification.
post to wall	Displays the response.
action scope : String	(Optional) Optional if identical to the scope requested by the client; otherwise, the scope of the access token as described by Section 3.3 of the OAuth 2.0 specification.

Figure 11-1 shows how to use the OAuth functionality provided by TouchDevelop in order to post a message to Facebook:

1. It builds a URL that will trigger the Facebook authentication process for your app, for a particular "scope" which defines what kind of permissions your app is requesting.
2. Then it sends the actual message with the text to post. Note how not only the message text is encoded in a URL, but also the access_token that was obtained by the earlier authentication call.

If you use a different web service, or want to post other kind of information, it might be the case that you need to pass the access_token in a header field of the web request, and you might have to send the payload in the body of a POST web request. Consult the documentation of the web service you want to use.

Figure 11-1: Post a message to Facebook with OAuth

```
// 1. Authenticate
var application id := "Put-Your-Facebook-App-Id-here"
var url := "https://www.facebook.com/dialog/oauth/"
url := url ‖ "?client_id=" ‖ web → url encode(application id)
url := url ‖ "&scope=" ‖ web → url encode("publish_stream")
var oauth res := web → oauth v2(url)

// 2. Send message
var message := "TouchDevelop is cool!"
url := "https://graph.facebook.com/me/feed"
url := url ‖ "?access_token=" ‖ oauth res → access token
url := url ‖ "&message=" ‖ web → url encode(message)
var request := web → create request(url)
var response := request → send
var rjs := response → content as json
var id := rjs → string("id")
("message id: " ‖ id) → post to wall
```

11.3   Libraries

The following TouchDevelop libraries already implement the OAuth 2.0 authentication for a number of APIs. Each library contains detailed instructions on how to register an application in order to use them. Just search for the name of a library in the add-library-reference dialog.

- Microsoft Live
- Facebook
- Google
- Yammer
- FourSquare
- Instagram
- Meetup

Figure 11-2 shows how to use the Facebook library provided by TouchDevelop in order to post a message on Facebook. Before you can use the △facebook expression, you must add a reference to the Facebook library in your script.

Figure 11-1: Using Facebook Library

```
action main ()
    var application id := "Put-Your-Facebook-App-Id-here"
    △facebook → initialize(application id, "publish_stream")
    var id := △facebook → post text("", "TouchDevelop is cool!")
    ("text id: " ‖ id) → post to wall
```

11.4   Advanced topics

11.4.1   Unique redirect URIs

Some OAuth providers, such as Microsoft Live, require unique redirect URIs with unique domain names for each application. In those cases the basic redirect URI that is just specific to your user id does not work. Instead, you can use the following redirect URI scheme:

    https://[rdid]-[userid].users.touchdevelop.com/oauth

where [rdid] is a unique identifier for the app ("redirect domain id", fewer than 64 lower case alphanumeric ASCII characters) that you can choose, and [userid] is your TouchDevelop user id as before.

```
oauth res := web → oauth v2(url ‖ "&tdredirectdomainid=[rdid]")
```

When passing the authentication URL to web→oauth v2, add a tdredirectdomainid query argument to specify your [rdid].

11.4.2 *State variable in redirect URI*

Some OAuth providers fail to pass the state argument in the redirect URI, and this breaks the TouchDevelop OAuth support. In such case, add a tdstateinredirecturi=true query argument to the authentication URL.

```
oauth res := web → oauth v2(url ‖ "&tdstateinredirecturi=true")
```

Appendix A
Editing TouchDevelop Scripts

This appendix provides a worked example of creating a TouchDevelop script using an editor which runs inside your browser. It cannot cover all the editor's features. Some experimentation is suggested for gaining familiarity with the editor. The script to be entered is shown in Figure A-1. It is published under the name rotor with code name /gtbd.

Figure A-1: The rotor program /gtbd

```
action main (
    speed : Number)
do
    ⊞ rate := speed
    ⊞ bd := media → create board(480)
    var sprite := ⊞ bd → create rectangle(360, 60)
    if speed > 0 then
        sprite → set color(colors → red)
    else
        sprite → set color(colors → blue)
    ⊞ bd → post to wall

event gameloop ()
    var sprite := ⊞ bd → at(0)
    var x := sprite → angle + ⊞ rate
    sprite → set angle(x)
    ⊞ bd → update on wall

data bd : Board
data rate : Number
```

A.1   The starting point

Once you have signed into the TouchDevelop website, your current webpage is a page with the URL https://www.touchdevelop.com/app/#. This webpage is known as *the hub*.

In the top left of the hub, there should be a collection of tiles under the heading *my scripts*. If you have previously created or downloaded some scripts, there will be tiles for the more recent ones. If you wish to edit one of these scripts, just tap its tile and then tap the large orange tile labeled *edit*. If you don't see a tile for your previously created or downloaded script, tap the tile labeled *See More* and the browser will display a webpage which contains tiles for many more scripts, plus a button at the end of the list which reads *load more*. Tapping that button performs as advertised, extending the list with more tiles plus a new *load more* button at the end.

For our example, we are creating a completely new script so we tap the tile labeled *Create Script*. This causes the browser to display a scrollable list of script templates. The top portion of the list is shown in Figure A-2. We should look through the list to see if there is a template for the kind of script we wish to create. For our example, we tap the template named *blank* because none of the other templates seems to be appropriate.

The browser now displays a textbox into which we should enter a name for the new script. A default name reading something like 'my script 5' has been provided in the textbox, but we will change it to read 'rotor'. Having entered that text, we tap the button labeled *create*.

The browser now displays the webpage for the TouchDevelop script editor. As seen in the screenshot shown in Figure A-3, the webpage is divided into three columns.

- A narrow left column contains buttons labeled *my scripts*, *run* and *undo*. That undo button is very useful because it undoes the effect of any editing action performed by mistake.
- A wider second column has a tile for the new script itself, tapping that tile brings up a script properties page where the name of the script can be changed, along with many other properties which are not needed until the script is finished.

There are several headings below the initial tile, one for each possible section of a script. Underneath heading, there would be a tile for every action, every page, every event ... which has been added to the script. At this point, there is only a tile for an action named *main*.

- The remainder of the browser window is devoted to the third column which is the editing window. When we start, that window holds the code for the *main* action. A minimal version of the action which does nothing has been provided in the template.

Figure A-2: The first few script templates

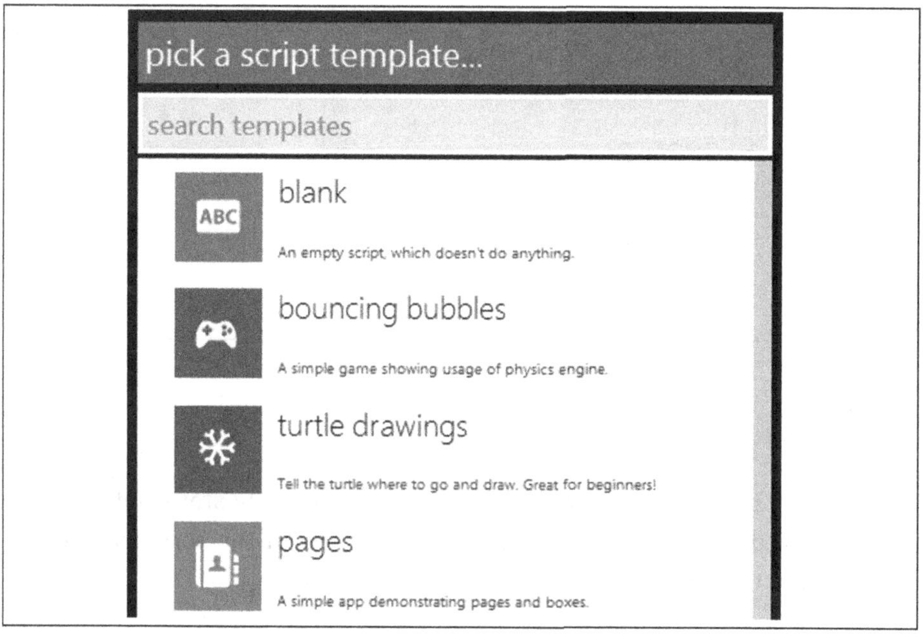

Figure A-3: The editor webpage

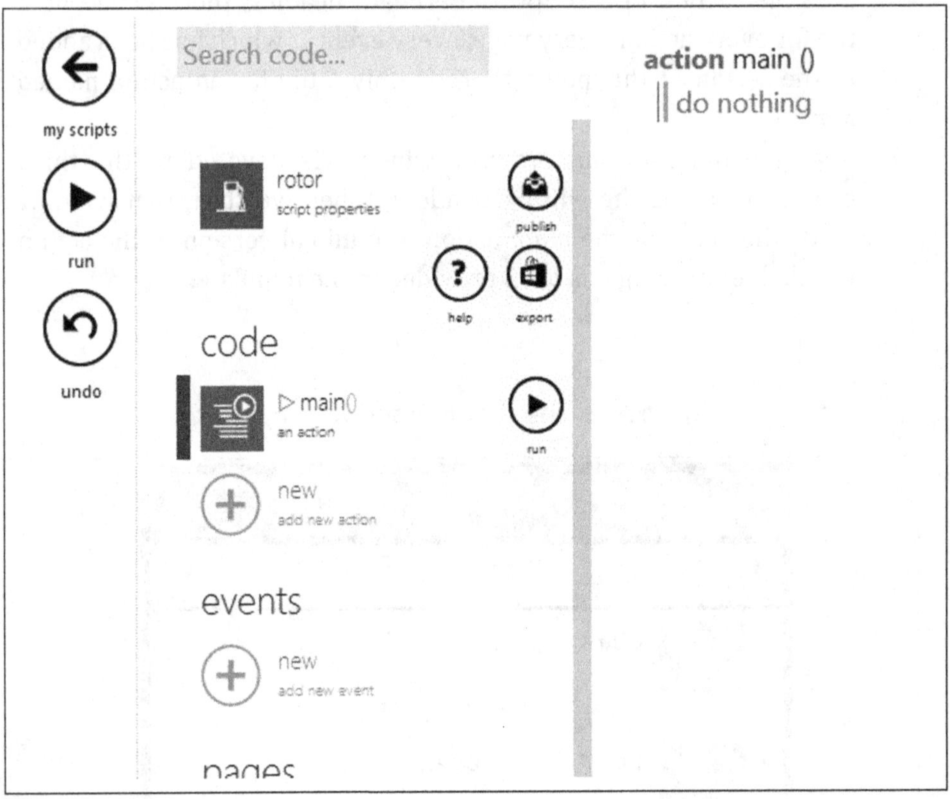

A.2   The editing steps

The screen contents change many times as the editing steps detailed below are followed. For space reasons, only a selection of the screenshots can be included in this appendix.

Getting started – providing an input parameter

The script for the main action will modified to have a parameter. Its code will then be as follows.

```
action main( speed : Number )
do
// do nothing
```

1. If the code for the main action is not displayed, tap on the tile for the main action underneath the code heading in the second column of

the main editor webpage (as in Figure A-3).

2. Our script needs an input parameter for its main action, so tap anywhere on the first line of the code for main – on the line which reads "action main()". That changes the second column of the webpage.

3. In the second column, there is a large gray plus symbol and the words "add input parameter". Tap that plus symbol. The code for main shown in the third hand column instantly changes to show an input parameter named p with type Number.

4. We do not want to keep the name p for that parameter, so tap anywhere in the line of code where p: Number appears. The webpage changes so that the second column displays details of parameter p and the third column indicates which part of the script we are focused on.

5. In the second column, the parameter's name p appears in a textbox whose contents can be edited. Select that name p using the mouse or a finger on a touchscreen, and enter the replacement name: speed. (The editor guessed the correct type for the parameter, so it does not need to be changed. If we had wanted a different type, tapping the tile for the Number type would allow us to select an alternative.) Tap anywhere in the third column, and the code is redisplayed showing the new parameter name.

Adding the first statement to the action

The first statement to be inserted is ▢rate := speed

1. Tap anywhere in the comment which reads *do nothing*. This causes the comment to disappear and be replaced with a vertical bar which indicates the insertion point for subsequent editing actions. More importantly, two keypads appear side-by-side at the bottom of the browser window. The two keypads are shown in Figure A-4 and Figure A-5. The left keypad is used for entering or editing constants (numbers, strings and Booleans). The right keypad is used for entering statements and expressions.

2. The top row of the right-hand keypad shows different kinds of statements. We wish to insert an assignment to a new variable, so

tap on the tile labeled *var*. The code changes to show an assignment to a new variable named x where the right-hand side is empty. The red bar is on the right side, indicating where the editor will insert new items. See Figure A-6. The right keypad at the bottom of the window also changed; it now shows only items which can appear at the current insertion point in the code.

3. One of the tiles in the keypad is labeled *speed*. Tap that tile. The identifier speed gets inserted into right side of the assignment.

4. The right side is complete, but the left side is not the variable we wanted. Select the left side of the assignment. This causes the insertion bar to appear just to the right of the name x. In addition, the right keypad at the bottom of the screen has changed again. There is a tile labeled rename. Tap it.

5. Enter the desired name *rate* on the keyboard. And then tap anywhere below on the screen. The code for the action is redisplayed showing the statement as var rate := speed.

6. We did not want rate to be a local variable, so tap anywhere in that statement and then tap the left hand side. The insertion bar appears alongside the name rate and the right keypad re-appears.

7. Tap the tile labeled promote to ☐data. This causes the code to be redisplayed, with the assignment now reading ☐rate := speed. The second column in the window has also changed; a global variable named rate has appeared in the data section of the script.

Figure A-4: The left keypad

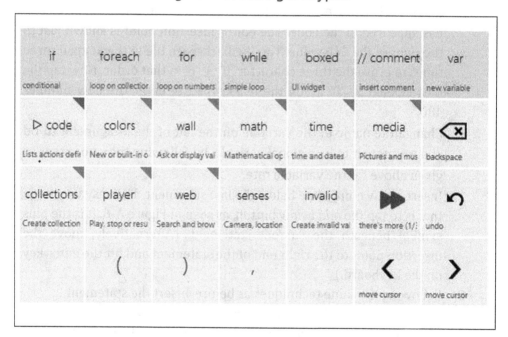

Figure A-5: The right keypad

Adding the second and third statements

The two statements to be inserted are as follows.

```
⊞bd := media→ create board(480)
var sprite := ⊞bd → create rectangle(360,60)
```

1. Tap on the right side of the previously inserted assignment

statement; this causes the insertion marker to appear after the identifier speed. Now hit the enter (or return) key. An empty line with the insertion marker at the left end appears.

2. Tap the *var* tile in the keypad to begin a new assignment statement to a new variable,

3. Tap the tile labeled *media*. There is one tile for each service or resource in the API. If you do not see the service you need, you can tap the special tile labeled "there's more". (It can be seen in Figure A-5.)

4. When the *media* tile was tapped, the identifier media appeared in the code for the statement and the keypad changed. The tiles in the keypad are now labeled with all the methods provided by the *media* service. Tap the *create board* tile.

5. A call to the create board method with a default parameter of 640 has appeared in the code. The editor insertion point is shown just to the right of the 640 value. Tap the backspace tile in the keypad three times to erase the three character '0' '4' '6' in that order. Now tap the tiles labeled '4' '8' '0' on the left keypad to enter the new number 480.

6. Change the name of the variable on the left of the assignment to bd and promote it to be a global variable, by following the same steps as given above for the variable rate.

7. Insert a new empty line below the last statement. The easy way to do that is to tap the *add below* button, as seen in Figure A-6. It is the plus symbol beneath the current statement. (Alternatively, move the insertion point to the right end of the statement and hit the enter key on the keyboard.)

8. Following the same techniques as before, insert the statement
   var sprite := ⊞bd → create rectangle(360,60)
   (To insert the global variable ⊞bd into the right side, look for the key labeled ⊞data on the keypad; after tapping that, there will be a key labeled bd, one for each global variable defined so far, and this should be tapped.)

Figure A-6: Add above and add below buttons

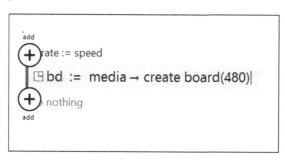

Inserting the if statement

The statements to be inserted are the following:

        if speed > 10 then
sprite → set color(colors → red)
else
        sprite → set color(colors → blue)
⊟bd → post to wall

1. Tap in the last statement entered and tap the *add below* button. Then tap the tile in the top row of the right keypad which is labeled *if*. An empty if-then-else statement is inserted into the script.
2. With the current insertion point at the place where the conditional expression should go, tap the key labeled speed in the right keypad. then tap the key labeled > and finally tap the key labeled 0 in the left keypad.
3. Tap on the *do nothing* comment in the *then* clause of the **if** statement and insert the initial version of the next statement by tapping keys labeled *sprite* and *set color*.
4. The new statement has colors→random as the argument of set color. Tap on the name random to select it. Then tap the tile labeled *backspace* in the right keypad to delete the →random part. Finally tap the tile labeled *red* in the right keypad.
5. Select the **else** keyword as the insertion point and similarly insert the statement sprite → set color(colors → blue).
6. Tap on the keyword **if** so that the whole **if** statement is enclosed within *add above* and *add below* buttons. Tap add below and the

insertion point becomes a new line below the **if** statement. Insert the final line ⊡bd→post to wall using steps similar to those previously described.

Defining the Gameloop Event

The final steps provide the code for the gameloop event. The code will read as follows.

```
event gameloop( )
         var sprite := ⊡bd → at(0)
         var x := sprite → angle + ⊡rate
         sprite → set angle(x)
         ⊡bd → update on wall
```

1. If necessary, tap anywhere in the window away from the recently entered code, so that the second column is displaying the different components of the script. There should be a heading which reads *events*. Tap the plus symbol below that heading.
2. A scrollable list of different kinds of events should be showing on the screen. Tap on the item labeled gameloop(). This new event will appear as one of the script's components in the second column, and the code for a *gameloop* event will appear in the third column.
3. Using the same kinds of steps as previously covered, the four statements to handle the event can be inserted.

Trying out the script

At this point, we should test the script.

1. The left column on the screen has a button labeled *run*. Tap this button to start the script running. Since the script requires an input parameter, a dialog box appears on the screen. Enter a number such as 10 into the text entry field and tap the OK button.
2. The display from the running script is like that in Figure A-7. To suspend the script, tap the *stop* button in the top right corner of the browser's window. To resume running the script, tap the button in the same spot as before (it has changed to be a *run* button).
3. To exit from the script's execution, tap the button in the top left

corner which is labeled with a left arrow. That will return to the editor.

Figure A-7: The running script

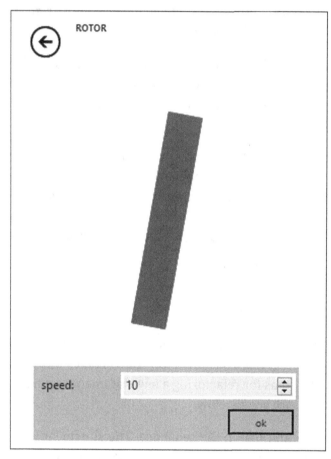

A.3   Additional steps

Revising the script

If the script does not behave as expected or needs improvement, it is easy to go back and edit the code. On the screen where the script components are listed, just tap the name of the action or the name of the event to display its code in the third column of the editor's window.

Publishing the script

If the code is something that is worth sharing with others, or simply to save it to the cloud, the script can be published. Just tap the upward pointing arrow, labeled *publish* underneath, which appears to the right of the tile for the script's properties in the second column.

After tapping the publish button, the screen should display a message with buttons underneath. One button is labeled *publish* and the other *publish as hidden*. The two buttons provide a choice of making the script visible or making it hidden.

If it is marked as visible, then anyone searching the TouchDevelop website for an example of a particular language feature or script feature may be directed to this script. It can also appear in lists of new scripts, or featured scripts. If it is marked as hidden, then it will not show up in such searches (but anyone knowing the codename for the script can still access it).

A.4   More advanced editing features

A.4.1   Refactoring code into a new action

Removing a sequence of statements and making a new action from them is known as refactoring. The TouchDevelop editor makes this process easy. To demonstrate, the steps for refactoring a few statements from the *main* action in the *rotor* script are given below.

1. Select the first line in the sequence. The statement which assigns to the variable sprite in the *main* action is shown as selected in Figure A-8

2. Tap the button labeled mark which appears to the right of the window. The code listing display changes to be like that seen in Figure A-9. The extent of the lines of code to be refactored is shown by the two thick red lines.

3. Now drag the bottom red line downwards until it is immediately below the last statement to be transferred to the refactored action. The screen should be showing a selected group of lines similar to that shown in Figure A-10.

4. In the second column displayed in the browser window, there are several headings and several buttons. Underneath the heading which reads "extract selection into action", enter a suitable name for the new action into the textbox, replacing the default name of *do stuff*. Figure A-11 shows that textbox after entering the new name *update sprite*.

5. Now tap that extract button and the new action is created. The refactored action is provided with whichever parameters are needed to allow it to work correctly. A statement is inserted into the main action, replacing the refactored code.

It should be observed that the marked group of statements could have been selected by first marking the last line and then moving the top horizontal red line upwards. Or any line in the group can be marked and both end point lines adjusted.

Figure A-8: Selecting the first line

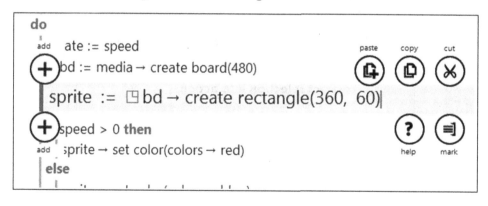

Figure A-9: Marking the first line to extract

```
bd := media → create board(480)
var sprite := bd → create rectangle(360, 60)
if speed > 0 then
   sprite → set color(colors → red)
else
   sprite → set color(colors → blue)
```

Figure A-10: Marking the last line to extract

```
bd := media → create board(480)
var sprite := bd → create rectangle(360, 60)
if speed > 0 then
   sprite → set color(colors → red)
else
   sprite → set color(colors → blue)
bd → post to wall
```

Figure A-11: Naming the extracted code

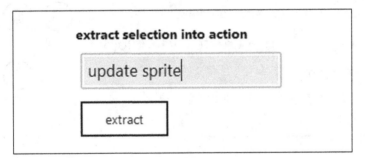

extract selection into action

update sprite

extract

A.4.2   Copying and pasting code

If a range of lines of code has been marked, following steps similar to those given above, those lines can be cut and temporarily held on the editor's clipboard.

Next another place in the code of any action or event can be selected. A button labeled *paste* appears on the right hand side. Tap that button to insert the cut code next to the selected line.

The pasted code appears above or below the selected line and which of the two places is chosen depends on various factors. To force the correct placement, always begin by inserting an empty line at the desired place for the pasted code. Then the *paste* button causes the pasted code to replace that empty line.

A.4.3   Surrounding code in a higher-level construct

Sometimes some complicated editing actions are needed. For example, an existing group of statements might need to become the **then** clause of a new **if** statement. That group of lines simply needs be marked using the same steps as previously described.

In the second column of the editor's window, there is a heading which reads "surround with" and underneath there are buttons labeled *if, for each, for, while* and *boxed*. Each one of these buttons performs exactly as advertised.

Appendix B
TouchDevelop Services

This appendix reproduces material found on the TouchDevelop website at https://www.touchdevelop.com/docs/api. It is provided here to make the book more self-contained. Appendix B covers the objects (known as *resources* or *services*) provided by the API. The datatypes are covered in Appendix C.

B.1   bazaar

Browse and review scripts from the bazaar.

ast of(id : String) : Json Object	Returns Abstract Syntax Tree JSON object for specified script
leaderboard score : Number	Gets the current score for the current script
post leaderboard score(score : Number)	Posts the current game score to the script leaderboard
post leaderboard to wall	Posts the current game leaderboard to the wall
script id(which : String) : String	Returns an identifier for either the top-level script or the current library

B.2   box

Access current box element on the page.

edit(style : String, value : String, changehandler : Text Action)	Display editable text, with the given binding
on tapped(handler : Action)	Set what happens when the box is tapped
page height : Number	Get the total height of the page
page width : Number	Get the total width of the page
pixels per em : Number	Get the number of pixels in an em
set background(color : Color)	Sets the background color

set border(color : Color, width : Number)	Set the color and width of the border
set border widths(top : Number, right : Number, bottom : Number, left : Number)	Set the width of each border
set font size(font size : Number)	Set font size in this box
set foreground(color : Color)	Sets the foreground color of elements
set height(height : Number)	Set the height of this box
set height range(min width : Number, max width : Number)	Set lower and upper limits on the width of this box
set horizontal align(arrange : String)	Specify how to arrange the content of this box; arrange is "left" "center" "right" or "justify"
set horizontal stretch(elasticity : Number)	Specify how to compute box width (0 = shrink to fit content, 1 = stretch to fit frame, 0.5 = stretch to half width
set margins(top : Number, right : Number, bottom : Number, left : Number)	Set the margins of this box (to leave space around the outside of this box)
set padding(top : Number, right : Number, bottom : Number, left : Number)	Set the padding of this box (to leave space around the contents of this box)
set scrolling(horizontal scrolling : Boolean, vertical scrolling : Boolean)	Specify whether to use scrollbars when box contents overflow
set text wrapping(wrap : Boolean, minimumwidth : Number)	Set whether to break long lines, and specify what length is too short for breaking
set vertical align(arrange : String)	Specify how to arrange the content of this box; arrange is "top" "bottom" "center" or "baseline"
set vertical stretch(elasticity : Number)	Specify how to compute box height (0 = shrink to fit content, 1 = stretch to fit frame, 0.5 = stretch to half height)
set width(width : Number)	Set the width of this box
set width range(min width : Number, max width : Number)	Set lower and upper limits on the width of this box
use horizontal layout	Arrange boxes inside this box from left to right
use overlay layout	Arrange boxes inside this box as layers on top of each other
use vertical layout	Arrange boxes inside this box from top to bottom; this is the default

B.3   collections

Create collections of items.

create link collection : Link Collection	Creates an empty link collection
create location collection : Location Collection	Creates an empty location collection
create message collection : Message Collection	Creates an empty message collection
create number collection : Number Collection	Creates an empty number collection
create number map : Number Map	Creates an empty number map
create place collection : Place Collection	Creates an empty place collection
create string collection : String Collection	Creates an empty string collection
create string map : String Map	Creates an empty string map (case and culture sensitive)

B.4   colors

Access predefined colors or create new colors.

accent : Color	Gets the accent color in the current theme
background : Color	Gets the background color in the current theme
black : Color	Gets the color that has the ARGB value of #FF000000
blue : Color	Gets the color that has the ARGB value of #FF0000FF
brown : Color	Gets the color that has the ARGB value of #FFA52A2A
chrome : Color	Gets the chrome color in the current theme (control background)
cyan : Color	Gets the color that has the ARGB value of #FF00FFFF
dark gray : Color	Gets the color that has the ARGB value of #FFA9A9A9
foreground : Color	Gets the foreground color in the current theme
from ahsb(alpha : Number, hue : Number, saturation : Number, brightness : Number) : Color	Creates a color from the alpha, hue, saturation, brightness channels (0.0-1.0 range)

from argb(alpha : Number, red : Number, green : Number, blue : Number) : Color	Creates a color from the alpha, red, green, blue channels (0.0-1.0 range)
from hsb(hue : Number, saturation : Number, brightness : Number) : Color	Creates a color from the hue, saturation, brightness channels (0.0-1.0 range)
from rgb(red : Number, green : Number, blue : Number) : Color	Creates a color from the red, green, blue channels (0.0-1.0 range)
gray : Color	Gets the color that has the ARGB value of #FF808080
green : Color	Gets the color that has the ARGB value of #FF008000
is light theme : Boolean	Indicates if the user is using a light theme in his phone
light gray : Color	Gets the color that has the ARGB value of #FFD3D3D3
linear gradient(c1 : Color, c2 : Color, alpha : Number) : Color	Computes an intermediate color
magenta : Color	Gets the color that has the ARGB value of #FFFF00FF
orange : Color	Gets the color that has the ARGB value of #FFFFA500
purple : Color	Gets the color that has the ARGB value of #FF800080
random : Color	Picks a random color
red : Color	Gets the color that has the ARGB value of #FFFF0000
sepia : Color	Gets the color that has the ARGB value of #FF704214
subtle : Color	Gets the subtle color in the current theme (light gray)
transparent : Color	Gets the color that has the ARGB value of #00FFFFFF
white : Color	Gets the color that has the ARGB value of #FFFFFFFF
yellow : Color	Gets the color that has the ARGB value of #FFFFFF00

B.5   contract

Statements that test whether correctness requirements are satisfied.

assert(condition : Boolean, message : String)	Checks for a condition; if the condition is false, execution fails. Does nothing for published scripts.
requires(condition : Boolean, message : String)	Specifies a precondition contract for the action; if the condition is false, execution fails. Does nothing for published scripts.

B.6   invalid

Create an invalid value for any datatype.

Action : Action	Creates an invalid Action instance
appointment : Appointment	Creates an invalid Appointment instance
appointment collection : Appointment Collection	Creates an invalid Appointment Collection instance
board : Board	Creates an invalid Board instance
boolean : Boolean	Creates an invalid Boolean instance
camera : Camera	Creates an invalid Camera instance
color : Color	Creates an invalid Color instance
contact : Contact	Creates an invalid Contact instance
contact collection : Contact Collection	Creates an invalid Contact Collection instance
datetime : DateTime	Creates an invalid DateTime instance
device : Device	Creates an invalid Device instance
device collection : Device Collection	Creates an invalid Device Collection instance
form builder : Form Builder	Creates an invalid Form Builder instance
json builder : Json Builder	Creates an invalid Json Builder instance
json object : Json Object	Creates an invalid Json Object instance
link : Link	Creates an invalid Link instance
link collection : Link Collection	Creates an invalid Link Collection instance
location : Location	Creates an invalid Location instance
location collection : Location Collection	Creates an invalid Location Collection instance
map : Map	Creates an invalid Map instance
Matrix : Matrix	Creates an invalid Matrix instance
media link : Media Link	Creates an invalid Media.Link instance

media link collection : Media Link Collection	Creates an invalid Media Link Collection instance
media player : Media Player	Creates an invalid Media Player instance
media player collection : Media Player Collection	Creates an invalid Media Player Collection instance
media server : Media Server	Creates an invalid Media Server instance
media server collection : Media Server Collection	Creates an invalid Media Server Collection instance
message : Message	Creates an invalid Message instance
message collection : Message Collection	Creates an invalid Message Collection instance
message collection action : Action	Creates an invalid Message Collection Action instance
motion : Motion	Creates an invalid Motion instance
number : Number	Creates an invalid Number instance
number collection : Number Collection	Creates an invalid Number Collection instance
number map : Number Map	Creates an invalid Number Map instance
oauth response : OAuth Response	Creates an invalid OAuth Response instance
page : Page	Creates an invalid Page instance
page button : Page Button	Creates an invalid Page Button instance
page collection : Page Collection	Creates an invalid Page Collection instance
picture : Picture	Creates an invalid Picture instance
picture album : Picture Album	Creates an invalid Picture Album instance
picture albums : Picture Albums	Creates an invalid Picture Albums instance
pictures : Pictures	Creates an invalid Pictures instance
place : Place	Creates an invalid Place instance
place collection : Place Collection	Creates an invalid Place Collection instance
playlist : Playlist	Creates an invalid Playlist instance
playlists : Playlists	Creates an invalid Playlists instance
position action : Action	Creates an invalid Position Action instance
song : Song	Creates an invalid Song instance
song album : Song Album	Creates an invalid Song Album instance
song albums : Song Albums	Creates an invalid Song Albums instance
songs : Songs	Creates an invalid Songs instance
sound : Sound	Creates an invalid Sound instance
sprite : Sprite	Creates an invalid Sprite instance
sprite action : Action	Creates an invalid Sprite Action instance
sprite set : Sprite Set	Creates an invalid Sprite Set instance
sprite set action : Action	Creates an invalid Sprite Set Action instance
string : String	Creates an invalid String instance
string collection : String Collection	Creates an invalid String Collection instance
string map : String Map	Creates an invalid String Map instance

text action : Action	Creates an invalid Text Action instance
textbox : TextBox	Creates an invalid TextBox instance
vector3 : Vector3	Creates an invalid Vector3 instance
vector action : Action	Creates an invalid Vector Action instance
web request : Web Request	Creates an invalid Web Request instance
web response : Web Response	Creates an invalid Web Response instance
webresponse action : Action	Creates an invalid WebResponse Action instance
xml object : Xml Object	Creates an invalid Xml Object instance

B.7 languages

Translation, and speech to text services.

current language : String	Gets the current language code, to be used in the 'translate' method
detect language(text : String) : String	Automatically detects the language of a given text using Bing.
picture to text(lang : String, pic : Picture) : String	Extracts text in the picture using Project Hawaii from Microsoft Research
record text : String	Converts the microphone dictation to text using Project Hawaii from Microsoft Research
speak(lang : String, text : String) : Sound	Speaks the text in the specified language using Bing
speech to text(lang : String, speech : Sound) : String	Converts a sound to a text using Project Hawaii from Microsoft Research
translate(source lang : String, target lang : String, text : String) : String	Translates some text between two languages using Bing. Empty source language to auto-detect

B.8 locations

Geo coordinates services.

create location(latitude : Number, longitude : Number) : Location	Creates a new geo coordinate location
create location list : Location Collection	Creates an empty list of locations
describe location(location : Location) : String	Looks for an address near a location using Bing
search location(address : String, postal code : String, city : String, country : String) : Location	Looks for the coordinate of an address using Bing

B.9   maps

Maps, location to address and address to location services.

create full map : Map	Creates a full screen Bing map. Use 'post to wall' to display it.
create map : Map	Creates a Bing map. Use 'post to wall' to display it.
directions(from : Location, to : Location, walking : Boolean) : Location Collection	Calculates the directions between two coordinates using Bing.
open directions(start search : String, start loc : Location, end search : String, end loc : Location)	Shows the directions in the Bing map application. If search term is provided, location is ignored. Provide search term or location for start and end.
open map(center : Location, search : String, zoom : Number)	Opens the Bing map application. zoom between 0 (close) and 1 (far)

B.10   math

Mathematical constants, operators, and functions such as cos, sin etc.

∞_- : Number	Returns negative infinity
∞_+ : Number	Returns positive infinity
abs(x : Number) : Number	Returns the absolute value of a number
acos(x : Number) : Number	Returns the angle whose cosine is the specified number
asin(x : Number) : Number	Returns the angle whose sine is the specified number
atan(x : Number) : Number	Returns the angle whose tangent is the specified number
atan2(y : Number, x : Number) : Number	Returns the angle whose tangent is the quotient of two specified numbers
ceiling(x : Number) : Number	Returns the smallest integral value greater than or equal to the specified number
cos(angle : Number) : Number	Returns the cosine of the specified angle
cosh(angle : Number) : Number	Returns the hyperbolic cosine of the specified angle
create matrix(rows : Number, columns : Number) : Matrix	Creates a matrix of zeros of a given size

create vector3(x : Number, y : Number, z : Number) : Vector3	Creates a 3D vector
deg to rad(degrees : Number) : Number	Converts degrees into radians
e : Number	Returns the natural logarithmic base, specified by the constant, e
ε : Number	Returns the machine epsilon, the smallest positive number greater than zero
exp(x : Number) : Number	Returns e raised to the specified power
floor(x : Number) : Number	Returns the largest integer less than or equal to the specified number
gravity : Number	Returns the value of standard gravity (9.80665) in meters/sec^2
ieee remainder(x : Number, y : Number) : Number	Returns the remainder resulting from the division of a specified number by another specified number
is ∞(x : Number) : Boolean	Indicates whether number evaluates to negative or positive infinity
is ∞_(x : Number) : Boolean	Indicates whether number evaluates to negative infinity
is ∞_+(x : Number) : Boolean	Indicates whether number evaluates to positive infinity
is nan(x : Number) : Boolean	Indicates that value cannot be represented as a number, i.e. Not-a-Number. This usually happens when the number is the result of a division by zero.
log(x : Number, base : Number) : Number	Returns the logarithm of a specified number in a specified base
log10(x : Number) : Number	Returns the base 10 logarithm of a specified number
loge(x : Number) : Number	Returns the natural (base e) logarithm of a specified number
max(x : Number, y : Number) : Number	Returns the larger of two numbers
min(x : Number, y : Number) : Number	Returns the smaller of two numbers
mod(x : Number, y : Number) : Number	Returns the modulus resulting from the division of one number by another number
π : Number	Returns the constant pi
pow(x : Number, y : Number) : Number	Returns a specified number raised to the specified power
rad to deg(radians : Number) : Number	Converts rad into degrees
random(max : Number) : Number	Returns a random integral number x: $0 \leq x < max$

random normalized : Number	Returns a random floating-point number x: 0 ≤ x < 1
round(x : Number) : Number	Rounds a number to the nearest integral value
round with precision(x : Number, digits : Number) : Number	Rounds a number to a specified number of fractional digits.
sign(x : Number) : Number	Returns a value indicating the sign of a number
sin(angle : Number) : Number	Returns the sine of the specified angle
sinh(angle : Number) : Number	Returns the hyperbolic sine of the specified angle
sqrt(x : Number) : Number	Returns the square root of a specified number
tan(angle : Number) : Number	Returns the tangent of the specified angle
tanh(angle : Number) : Number	Returns the hyperbolic tangent of the specified angle

B.11   media

Pictures and music.

choose picture : Picture	Chooses a picture from the media library
choose song : Song	Chooses a song from the media library (planned addition to the API)
create board(height : Number) : Board	Creates a new game board
create landscape board(width: Number, height : Number) : Board	Creates a new game board in landscape mode. On rotatable devices it will take the entire screen when posted.
create picture(width : Number, height : Number) : Picture	Creates a new picture of the given size
create portrait board(width: Number, height : Number) : Board	Creates a new game board in portrait mode. On rotatable devices it will take the entire screen when posted.
picture albums : Picture Albums	Gets the picture albums
pictures : Pictures	Gets the pictures on the phone
playlists : Playlists	Gets the playlists on the phone
saved pictures : Pictures	Gets the saved pictures on the phone
search marketplace(terms : String, type : String)	Searches the Windows Phone Marketplace (type in applications or music)
song albums : Song Albums	Gets the song albums on the phone
songs : Songs	Gets the songs on the phone

B.12 phone

Phone numbers, vibrate, etc.

choose address : Link	Chooses an address from the contacts
choose phone number : Link	Chooses a phone number from the contact list
dial phone number(number : String)	Starts a phone call
power source : String	Indicates if the phone is on 'battery' or 'external' power source.
save phone number(phone number : String)	Allows the user to save the phone number
vibrate(seconds : Number)	Vibrates the phone for a number of seconds (0.02 minimum)

B.13 player

Play, stop or resume songs

active song : Song	Gets the active song if any
is muted : Boolean	Indicates if the player is muted
is paused : Boolean	Indicates if the player is paused
is playing : Boolean	Indicates if the player is playing a song
is repeating : Boolean	Indicates if the player is repeating
is shuffled : Boolean	Indicates if the player is shuffled
is stopped : Boolean	Indicates if the player is stopped
next	Moves to the next song in the queue of playing songs
pause	Pauses the currently playing song
play(song : Song)	Plays a Song
play home media(media : Media Link)	Plays an audio/video file from the home network
play many(songs : Songs)	Plays a collection of songs
play position : Number	Gets the position in seconds within the active song
previous	Moves to the previous song in the queue of playing songs
resume	Resumes a paused song
set repeating(repeating : Boolean)	Sets the repeating on and off

set shuffled(shuffled : Boolean)	Sets the shuffling on and off
set sound volume(x : Number)	Sets the sound volume level from 0 (silent) to 1 (current volume)
sound volume : Number	Gets the sound volume for sounds from 0 (silent) to 1 (current volume)
stop	Stops playing a song

B.14   senses

Camera, location, microphone and other sensors.

acceleration quick : Vector3	Gets filtered accelerometer data using a combination of a low-pass and threshold triggered high-pass on each axis to eliminate the majority of the sensor low amplitude noise while trending very quickly to large offsets (not perfectly smooth signal in that case), providing a very low latency. This is ideal for quickly reacting UI updates.
acceleration smooth : Vector3	Gets filtered accelerometer data using a 1 Hz first-order low-pass on each axis to eliminate the main sensor noise while providing a medium latency. This can be used for moderately reacting UI updates requiring a very smooth signal.
acceleration stable : Vector3	Gets filtered and temporally averaged accelerometer data using an arithmetic mean of the last 25 'optimally filtered' samples, so over 500ms at 50Hz on each axis, to virtually eliminate most sensor noise. This provides a very stable reading but it has also a very high latency and cannot be used for rapidly reacting UI.
battery level : Number	Gets the charge level of the battery between 0 (discharged) and 1 (fully charged). Returns invalid if this information is not available.
camera : Camera	Gets the primary camera
current location : Location	Gets the current phone location. The phone optimizes the accuracy for power, performance, and other cost considerations.
current location accurate : Location	Gets the current phone location with the most accuracy. This includes using services that might charge money, or consuming higher levels of battery power or connection bandwidth.
front camera : Camera	Gets the front facing camera
has gyroscope : Boolean	Indicates if the gyroscope is available on the device

heading : Number	Gets the compass heading, in degrees, measured clockwise from the Earth's geographic north.
is device stable : Boolean	Indicates whether the device is 'stable' (no movement for about 0.5 seconds)
motion : Motion	Gets the current phone motion that combines data from the accelerometer, compass and gyroscope.
orientation : Vector3	Gets the current orientation in degrees if available. (x,y,z) is also called (pitch, roll, yaw) or (alpha, beta, gamma).
record microphone : Sound	Records audio using the microphone
rotation speed : Vector3	Gets the gyroscope rotational velocity around each axis of the device, in degrees per second.
take camera picture : Picture	Takes a picture and returns it. This picture does not contain the gps location.

B.15   social

Emails, sms, contacts, and calendar services.

choose contact : Contact	Chooses a contact from the contact list
choose email : Link	Chooses an email from the contact list
create contact(nickname : String) : Contact	Creates a new contact
create message(message : String) : Message	Creates a message to share
create place(name : String, location : Location) : Place	Creates a place
link email(email address : String) : Link	Creates a link from an email
link phone number(phone number : String) : Link	Creates a link from a phone number
save contact(contact : Contact)	Saves a new contact
save email(email address : String)	Allows the user to save the email address (email)
search(network : String, terms : String) : Message Collection	Searches for recent messages in a social network (twitter, facebook)
search appointments(start : DateTime, end : DateTime) : Appointment Collection	Searches for appointments in a given time range
search contacts(prefix : String) : Contact Collection	Searches for contacts by name.
search places nearby(network : String, terms : String, location : Location, distance : Number) : Place Collection	Searches for places nearby. The distance is in meters.
send email(to : String, subject : String, body : String)	Opens the mail client

send sms(to : String, body : String)	Opens the short message client (to, body)

B.16   tags

2D barcodes, QR codes and NFC tags..

send nfc(value : String, type : String)	Sends a url or text using NFC
tag text(text : String, size : Number, bw : Boolean) : Picture	Generates a 2D barcode pointing to the text using Microsoft Tag. text must be less than 1000 character long and size must be between 0.75 and 5 inches.
tag url(url : String, size : Number, bw : Boolean) : Picture	Generates a 2D barcode pointing to the url using Microsoft Tag. url must be less than 1000 character long and size must be between 0.75 and 5 inches

B.17   tile

Windows 8 and Windows phones have tiles displayed on the start screen which initiate an application program when tapped. A tile may be associated with a TouchDevelop script through use of this service. Note: this resource replaces the Tile datatype which is no longer supported.

pin default	prompt the user whether a tile should be pinned to the start screen

set default counter(n : Number)	Set a counter (a number) which is displayed on the tile; only values in the range 1 to 99 are displayed; other values are hidden
set default text(title: String, text : String)	Displays a short title and a longer piece of text on the tile

B.18   time

Time and date operations.

create(year : Number, month : Number, day : Number, hour : Number, minute : Number, second : Number) : DateTime	Creates a new date instance
fail if not(condition : Boolean)	Aborts the execution if the condition is false.
log(message : String)	Appends this message to the debug log. Does nothing when the script is published.
now : DateTime	Gets the current time
sleep(seconds : Number)	Waits for a specified amount of seconds
stop	Stops the execution and stays on the wall.
today : DateTime	Gets today's date without time
tomorrow : DateTime	Gets tomorrow's date without time

B.19   wall

Ask for or display values on the wall.

add button(icon : String, text : String) : Page Button	Add a new button. icon must be the name of a built-in icon, text must be non-empty.
ask boolean(text : String, caption : String) : Boolean	Prompts the user with ok and cancel buttons
ask number(text : String) : Number	Prompts the user to input a number
ask string(text : String) : String	Prompts the user to input a string

button icon names : String Collection	Gets the list of available page button names.
clear	Clears the background, buttons and entries
clear background	Clears the background color, picture and camera
clear buttons	Clears the application bar buttons and hides the bar
create text box(text : String, font size : Number) : TextBox	Creates an updatable text box
current page : Page	Gets the current page displayed on the wall
display search(on : Boolean)	Indicates whether to show or hide the search icon
pages : Page Collection	Returns the current back stack of pages, starting from the current page to the bottom page.
pick date(text : String, caption : String) : DateTime	Prompts the user to pick a date. Returns a datetime whose date is set, the time is 12:00:00.
pick string(text : String, caption : String, values : String Collection) : Number	Prompts the user to pick a string from a list. Returns the selected index.
pick time(text : String, caption : String) : DateTime	Prompts the user to pick a time. Returns a datetime whose time is set, the date is undefined.
pop page : Boolean	Pops the current page and restores the previous wall page. Returns false if already on the default page.
prompt(text : String)	Prompts the user with an ok button
push new page : Page	Pushes an empty page on the wall
screenshot : Picture	Takes a screenshot of the wall
set background(color : Color)	Sets the wall background color
wall→set background camera(camera : Camera)	Sets the wall background camera
set background picture(picture : Picture)	Sets the wall background picture. The picture will be resized and clipped to the screen background as needed
set foreground(color : Color)	Sets the wall foreground color of elements
set reversed(bottom : Boolean)	Reverses the elements on the wall and inserts new ones at the bottom.
set subtitle(title : String)	Sets the subtitle of the wall
set title(title : String)	Sets the title of the wall
set transform matrix(m11 : Number, m12 : Number, m21 : Number, m22 : Number, offsetx : Number, offsety : Number)	Sets the 3x3 affine matrix transformation applied to the wall

B.20   web

Search and browse the web.

base64 decode(text : String) : String	Decodes a string that has been base64-encoded
base64 encode(text : String) : String	Converts a string into an base64-encoded string
browse(url : String)	Opens a web browser to a url
connection name : String	Gets a name of the currently connected network servicing Internet requests
connection type : String	Gets the type of the network servicing Internet requests (unknown, none, ethernet, wifi, mobile)
create form builder : Form Builder	Create a form builder
create json builder : Json Builder	Creates a json builder
create request(url : String) : Web Request	Creates a web request
csv(text : String, delimiter : String) : Json Object	Parses a Command Separated Values document into a JsonObject where the headers is a string array of column names; records is an array of rows where each row is itself an array of strings. The delimiter is inferred if not specified.
download(url : String) : String	Downloads the content of an internet page (http get)
download json(url : String) : Json Object	Downloads a web service response as a JSON data structure (http get)
download picture(url : String) : Picture	Downloads a picture from internet
download song(url : String, name : String) : Song	Create a streamed song file from internet (download happens when playing)
download sound(url : String) : Sound	Downloads a WAV sound file from internet
feed(value : String) : Message Collection	Parses the newsfeed string (RSS 2.0 or Atom 1.0) into a message collection
html decode(html : String) : String	Decodes a string that has been HTML-encoded
html encode(text : String) : String	Converts a text string into an HTML-encoded string
is connected : Boolean	Indicates whether any network connection is available
json(value : String) : Json Object	Parses the string as a json object

json array : Json Object	Returns an empty json array
json object : Json Object	Returns an empty json object
link image(url : String) : Link	Creates a link to an internet image
link media(url : String) : Link	Creates a link to an internet audio/video
link url(name : String, url : String) : Link	Creates a link to an internet page
oauth v2(oauth url : String) : OAuth Response	Authenticate with OAuth 2.0 and receive the access token or error. (See oauthv2 for more information on which Redirect URI to choose.)
open connection settings(page : String)	Opens a connection settings page (airplanemode, bluetooth, wiki, cellular)
play media(url : String)	Plays an internet audio/video in full screen
search(terms : String) : Link Collection	Search the web using Bing
search images(terms : String) : Link Collection	Search for images using Bing
search images nearby(terms : String, location : Location, distance : Number) : Link Collection	Search for images near a location using Bing. Distance in meters, negative to ignore.
search nearby(terms : String, location : Location, distance : Number) : Link Collection	Searching the web near a location using Bing. Distance in meters, negative to ignore.
search news(terms : String) : Link Collection	Search for news using Bing
search news nearby(terms : String, location : Location, distance : Number) : Link Collection	Search for news near a location using Bing. Distance in meters, negative to ignore.
upload(url : String, body : String) : String	Uploads text to an internet page (http post)
upload picture(url : String, pic : Picture) : String	Uploads a picture to an internet page (http post)
url decode(url : String) : String	Decodes a string that has been url-encoded
url encode(text : String) : String	Converts a text string into an url-encoded string
xml(value : String) : Xml Object	Parses the string as a xml element

Appendix C
TouchDevelop Datatypes

This appendix reproduces material found on the TouchDevelop website at https://www.touchdevelop.com/docs/api. This appendix provides descriptions of the datatypes implemented in TouchDevelop. Appendix B covers *services* (also called *resources*).

C.1 Appointment

A value of this type describes one calendar appointment.

attendees : Contact Collection	Gets the list of attendees. Each contact contains a name and email address.
details : String	Gets the details
end time : DateTime	Gets the end time
is all day event : Boolean	Indicates if this is an all day event
is invalid : Boolean	Returns true if the current instance is useless
is private : Boolean	Indicates if this appointment is private
location : String	Gets the location
organizer : Contact	Gets the organizer
post to wall	Posts the appointment to the wall
source : String	Gets the source of this appointment (Facebook, etc...)
start time : DateTime	Gets the location
status : String	Gets your status (free, tentative, busy, outofoffice)
subject : String	Gets the subject

C.2 Appointment Collection

A value of this type represents a collection of appointments.

at(index : Number) : Appointment	Gets the appointment at index
count : Number	Gets the number of appointments
is invalid : Boolean	Returns true if the current instance is useless
post to wall	Posts the appointments on the wall

C.3 Board

An instance of the Board is a 2D image containing sprites and other graphic objects displayed by a games program.

at(i : Number) : Sprite	Gets the sprite indexed by i
clear background camera	Clears the background camera
clear background picture	Clear the background picture
clear events	Clear all queued events related to this board
count : Number	Gets the sprite count
create anchor(width : Number, height : Number) : Sprite	Create an anchor sprite
create boundary(distance : Number)	Create walls around the board at the given distance
create ellipse(width : Number, height : Number) : Sprite	Create a new ellipse sprite
create obstacle(x : Number, y : Number, x segment : Number, y segment : Number, elasticity : Number)	Create a line obstacle with given start point, and given extent. Elasticity is 0 for sticky, 1 for complete bounce.
create picture(picture : Picture) : Sprite	Create a new picture sprite.
create rectangle(width : Number, height : Number) : Sprite	Create a new rectangle sprite
create spring(sprite1 : Sprite, sprite2 : Sprite, stiffness : Number)	Create a spring between the two sprites
create sprite set : Sprite Set	Create a new collection for sprites
create text(width : Number, height : Number, fontSize : Number, text : String) : Sprite	Create a new text sprite.
evolve	Update positions of sprites on board.
height : Number	Gets the height in pixels
is invalid : Boolean	Returns true if the current instance is useless
is landscape : Boolean	Gets a value indicating if the board is designed to be viewed in landscape mode
post to wall	Shows the board on the wall.
set background(color : Color)	Sets the background color
set background camera(camera : Camera)	Sets the background camera
set background picture(picture : Picture)	Sets the background picture
set debug mode(debug : Boolean)	In debug mode, board displays speed and other info of sprites

set friction(friction : Number)	Sets the default friction for sprites to a fraction of speed loss between 0 and 1
set gravity(x : Number, y : Number)	Sets the uniform acceleration vector for objects on the board to pixels/sec^2
touch current : Vector3	Current touch point
touch end : Vector3	Last touch end point
touch start : Vector3	Last touch start point
touch velocity : Vector3	Final touch velocity after touch ended
touched : Boolean	True if board has been touched
update on wall	Make updates visible.
width : Number	Gets the width in pixels

C.4   Boolean

The datatype which has true or false as its two values.

and(right : Boolean) : Boolean	Builds conjunction
equals(right : Boolean) : Boolean	Indicates that the two values are equal
is invalid : Boolean	Returns true if the current instance is useless
not : Boolean	Negates the Boolean expression
or(right : Boolean) : Boolean	Builds disjunction
post to wall	Displays the value on the wall
to json : Json Object	Converts the value into a json data structure
to number : Number	Converts true to 1 and false to 0
to string : String	Converts a Boolean to a string

C.5   Camera

The front or back camera.

height : Number	Gets the height of the camera image in pixels
is front : Boolean	Returns false if this is the primary camera, and true otherwise
is invalid : Boolean	Returns true if the current instance is useless
post to wall	Displays the camera video stream in full screen
preview : Picture	Takes a low quality picture from the camera
width : Number	Gets the width of the camera image in pixels

C.6   Color

An argb color (alpha, red, green, blue)

A : Number	Gets the alpha value (0.0-1.0)
B : Number	Gets the blue value (0.0-1.0)
blend(other : Color) : Color	Composes a new color using alpha blending
brightness : Number	Gets the brightness component of the color
darken(delta : Number) : Color	Makes a darker color by a delta between 0 and 1
equals(other : Color) : Boolean	Checks if the color is equal to the other
G : Number	Gets the green value (0.0-1.0)
hue : Number	Gets the hue component of the color
is invalid : Boolean	Returns true if the current instance is useless
lighten(delta : Number) : Color	Makes a lighter color by a delta between 0 and 1
make transparent(alpha : Number) : Color	Creates a new color by changing the alpha channel from 0 (transparent) to 1 (opaque)
post to wall	Prints the value to the wall
R : Number	Gets the red value (0.0-1.0)
saturation : Number	Gets the saturation component of the color

C.7   Contact

An instance of this type represents a personal contact. The list of methods has been divided into three sections: *get methods* (which retrieve a single attribute of a contact), *set methods* (which set or update a single attribute), and *other methods*.

Get Methods of Contact Type	
birthday : DateTime	Gets the birth date if any.
company : String	Gets the company name if any.
email : Link	Gets the work or personal email if any
first name : String	Gets the first name if any.
home address : String	Gets the work address if any
home phone : Link	Gets the home phone number if any
job title : String	Gets the job title at the company if any.
last name : String	Gets the last name if any
middle name : String	Gets the middle name if any
mobile phone : Link	Gets the cell phone number if any
name : String	Gets the display name (not used when saving contact)
nick name : String	Gets the nickname if any
office : String	Gets the office location at the company if any
personal email : Link	Gets the personal email if any
phone number : Link	Gets the cell or work or home phone number if any

picture : Picture	Gets the picture of the contact if any
source : String	Gets the source of this contact (phone, etc...)
suffix : String	Gets the name suffix if any
title : String	Gets the name title if any
web site : Link	Gets the web site if any
work address : String	Gets the home address if any
work email : Link	Gets the work email if any
work phone : Link	Gets the work phone number if any

Set Methods of Contact Type	
set company(value : String)	Sets the company
set first name(value : String)	Sets the first name
set home phone(home phone : String)	Sets the home phone
set job title(value : String)	Sets the job title
set last name(value : String)	Sets the last name
set middle name(middle name : String)	Sets the middle name
set mobile phone(value : String)	Sets the mobile phone
set personal email(value : String)	Sets the personal email
set source(value : String)	Sets the source
set suffix(value : String)	Sets the suffix
set title(value : String)	Sets the title
set web site(value : String)	Sets the web site
set work email(value : String)	Sets the work email
set work phone(work phone : String)	Sets the work phone

Other Methods of Contact Type	
is invalid : Boolean	Returns true if the current instance is useless
post to wall	Posts the contact to the wall

C.8   Contact Collection

A collection of contacts

at(index : Number) : Contact	Gets the contact at index
count : Number	Gets the number of contacts
is invalid : Boolean	Returns true if the current instance is useless
post to wall	Posts the contacts on the wall

C.9   DateTime

A DateTime value is a combination of date and time. The list of methods has been separated into a table of *get methods* (which return a single attribute) and *other methods*.

Get Methods of DateTime Type	
date : DateTime	Gets the date
day : Number	Gets the day of the month
hour : Number	Gets the hour
millisecond : Number	Gets the millisecond
minute : Number	Gets the minute
month : Number	Gets the month
second : Number	Gets the second
week day : Number	Gets the day of the week (sunday = 0, monday = 1, ... saturday = 6)
year : Number	Gets the year
year day : Number	Gets the day of the year between 1 and 366

Other Methods of DateTime Type	
add days(days : Number) : DateTime	Returns a date that adds the specified number of days to the value of this instance
add hours(hours : Number) : DateTime	Returns a date that adds the specified number of hours to the value of this instance
add milliseconds(milliseconds : Number) : DateTime	Returns a date that adds the specified number of milliseconds to the value of this instance
add minutes(minutes : Number) : DateTime	Returns a date that adds the specified number of minutes to the value of this instance
add months(months : Number) : DateTime	Returns a date that adds the specified number of months to the value of this instance
add seconds(seconds : Number) : DateTime	Returns a date that adds the specified number of seconds to the value of this instance
add years(years : Number) : DateTime	Returns a date that adds the specified number of years to the value of this instance
equals(other: DateTime): Boolean	Compares dates for equality
greater(other: DateTime): Boolean	Compares dates for greater
greater or equal(other : DateTime) : Boolean	Compares dates for greater or equal
is invalid : Boolean	Returns true if the current instance is useless
less(other : DateTime) : Boolean	Compares dates for less

less or equals(other : DateTime) : Boolean	Compares dates for less or equal
not equals(other : DateTime) : Boolean	Compares dates for inequality
post to wall	Prints the date to the wall
subtract(value: DateTime): Number	Computes difference between date-times in seconds
to local time : DateTime	Converts to the local time
to json : Json Object	Converts the value into a json data structure
to local time : DateTime	Converts to the local time
to string : String	Converts a dates to a string
to universal time : DateTime	Converts coordinated universal time

C.10 Form Builder

A builder to create HTML Form data.

add boolean(name : String, value : Boolean)	Adds a boolean value
add number(name : String, value : Number)	Adds a number value
add picture(name : String, value : Picture, picture Name : String)	Adds a picture
add string(name : String, value : String)	Adds a string value
is invalid : Boolean	Returns true if the current instance is useless
post to wall	Posts the form to the wall

C.11 Json Builder

A json data structure builder.

add(value : Json Object)	Adds a value to the array
add null	Adds a null value to the array
is invalid : Boolean	Returns true if the current instance is useless
set boolean(name : String, value : Boolean)	Sets the boolean value
set field(name : String, value : Json Object)	Sets the field value
set field null(name : String)	Sets the field value as null
set number(name : String, value : Number)	Sets the number value

set string(name : String, value : String)	Sets the string value
to json : Json Object	Converts the builder into a json data structure and clears the builder

C.12   Json Object

A JSON data structure

at(index : Number) : Json Object	Gets the i-th json value
boolean(key : String) : Boolean	Gets a field value as a Boolean
contains key(key: String) : Boolean	Indicates if the key exists
count : Number	Gets the number of values
field(key : String) : Json Object	Gets a value by name
is invalid : Boolean	Returns true if the current instance is useless
keys : String Collection	Gets the list of keys
kind : String	Gets json kind (string, number, object, array, boolean)
number(key : String) : Number	Gets a field value as a number
post to wall	Prints the value to the wall
string(key : String) : String	Gets a field value as a string
time(key : String) : DateTime	Gets the field value as a time
to boolean : Boolean	Converts to a Boolean (type must be boolean)
to number : Number	Converts to a number (type must be number)
to string : String	Converts to a string (type must be string)
to time : DateTime	Converts and parses to a date time (type must be string)

C.13   Link

A link to a video, image, email, or a phone number.

address : String	Gets the url
is invalid : Boolean	Returns true if the current instance is useless
kind : String	Gets the kind of asset - media, image, email, phone number, hyperlink, deep zoom link, radio
location : Location	Gets the location if any
name : String	Gets the name if any
post to wall	Displays the link on the wall
set location(location : Location)	Sets the location
set name(name : String)	Sets the name

share(network : String)	Shares the link (email, sms, Facebook, social or " to pick from a list)

C.14   Link Collection

A list of links.

add(value : Link)	Adds a link
add many(value : Link Collection)	Adds many links at once
at(index : Number) : Link	Gets the i-th link
clear	Clears the collection
count : Number	Gets the number of elements
index of(item : Link, start : Number) : Number	Gets the index of the first occurrence of item. Returns -1 if not found or start is out of range.
insert at(index : Number, item : Link)	Inserts a link at position index. Does nothing if index is out of range.
is invalid : Boolean	Returns true if the current instance is useless
post to wall	Displays the links on the wall
random : Link	Gets a random element from the collection. Returns invalid if the collection is empty.
remove(item : Link) : Boolean	Removes the first occurrence of the link. Returns true if removed.
remove at(index : Number)	Removes the link at position index.
reverse	Reverses the order of the elements.
set at(index : Number, value : Link)	Sets the i-th link

C.15   Location

A geo coordinate (latitude, longitude, ...)

altitude : Number	Gets the altitude of the coordinate
course : Number	Gets the course of the coordinate
distance(other : Location) : Number	Calculates the distance in meters
equals(other : Location) : Boolean	Indicates if this instance is equal to the other
hor accuracy : Number	Gets the horizontal accuracy of the coordinate
is invalid : Boolean	Returns true if the current instance is useless
latitude : Number	Gets the latitude of the coordinate
longitude : Number	Gets the longitude of the coordinate
post to wall	Displays the location in a map using Bing
share(network : String, message : String)	Shares the location (email, sms, Facebook, social or " to pick from a list)
speed : Number	Gets the speed of the coordinate
to string : String	Converts to a string lat,long

| vert accuracy : Number | Gets the vertical accuracy of the coordinate |

C.16 Location Collection

add(value : Location)	Adds a location
add many(value : Location Collection)	Adds many locations at once
at(index : Number) : Location	Gets the i-th geo coordinate
clear	Clears the collection
count : Number	Gets the number of elements
index of(item : Location, start : Number) : Number	Gets the index of the first occurrence of item. Returns -1 if not found or start is out of range.
insert at(index : Number, item : Location) : Nothing	Inserts a location at position index. Does nothing if index is out of range.
is invalid : Boolean	Returns true if the current instance is useless
post to wall	Displays the locations in a map using Bing
random : Location	Gets a random element from the collection. Returns invalid if the collection is empty.
remove(item : Location) : Boolean	Removes the first occurrence of the location. Returns true if removed.
remove at(index: Number)	Removes the location at position index
reverse	Reverses the order of the elements
set at(index : Number, value : Location)	Sets the i-th geo coordinate
sort by distance(loc : Location)	Sorts by distance to the location

C.17 Map

A Bing map.

add line(locations : Location Collection, color : Color, thickness : Number)	Adds a polyline that passes through various geo coordinates
add link(link : Link, background : Color, foreground : Color)	Adds a link pushpin on the map (ignored if the location if not set)
add message(msg : Message, background : Color, foreground : Color)	Adds a message pushpin on the map (ignored if the location is not set)
add picture(location : Location, picture : Picture, background : Color)	Adds a picture pushpin on the map
add place(place : Place, background : Color, foreground : Color)	Adds a place pushpin on the map (ignored if the location is not set)

add text(location : Location, text : String, background : Color, foreground : Color)	Adds a text pushpin on the map
center : Location	Gets the map center location
clear	Clears the lines, regions and pushpins
fill region(locations : Location Collection, fill : Color, stroke : Color, thickness : Number)	Fills a region with a color
is invalid : Boolean	Returns true if the current instance is useless
post to wall	Displays the map in the wall using Bing
set center(center : Location)	Sets the map center location
set zoom(level : Number)	Sets the zoom level from 1 (earth) to 21 (street)
view pushpins	Changes the current zoom and center so that all the pushpins are visible. This method has no effect if the map is not posted on the wall yet.
zoom : Number	Gets the zoom level

C.18 Matrix

A two-dimensional matrix of numbers.

add(b : Matrix) : Matrix	Returns a matrix resulting from adding this matrix to b. The sizes of both matrices must match.
at(index : Number) : Number	Gets the value at a given index. Elements are ordered line by line starting top left.
clear(value : Number)	Sets all the element of the matrix to the value.
clone : Matrix	Creates a deep copy of the matrix.
column count : Number	Gets the number of columns
count : Number	Gets the total number of elements
is invalid : Boolean	Returns true if the current instance is useless
item(row : Number, column : Number) : Number	Gets the value at a given location. Returns invalid if outside the array dimensions.
max : Number	Computes the maximum of the values
min : Number	Computes the minimum of the values
multiply(b : Matrix) : Matrix	Returns a matrix resulting from multiplying each element in the matrices. The sizes of both matrices must match.
negate : Matrix	Returns the matrix negated.
post to wall	Displays the map in the wall using Bing

random : Number	Gets a random element. Returns invalid if the matrix is empty.
row count : Number	Gets the number of rows
scale(factor : Number) : Matrix	Returns a copy of the matrix scaled by factor
set at(index : Number, value : Number)	Sets the value at a given index. Elements are ordered line by line starting top left.
set item(row : Number, column : Number, value : Number)	Sets the value at a particular position. The matrix will be expanded with zero values if the position falls outside the boundaries.
subtract(b : Matrix) : Matrix	Returns a matrix resulting from subtracting b from this matrix. The sizes of both matrices must match.
to string : String	Gets the string representation of the matrix
transpose : Matrix	Returns the transposed matrix

C.19 Message

A Message value contains the details of a posting on a message board. The list of methods is separated into *get methods* (which retrieve a single attribute of a message), *set methods* (which assign or update an attribute value), and *other methods*.

Get Methods of Message Type	
from : String	Gets the author
id : String	Gets the message identifier
link : String	Gets the link associated with the message
location : Location	Gets the geo coordinates
media link : String	Gets a url to the media
message : String	Gets the message text
picture link : String	Gets a url for the picture
source : String	Gets the source of this message (Facebook, Twitter, etc...)
time : DateTime	Gets the time
title : String	Gets the title text
to : String	Gets the recipient
values : String Map	Gets additional values stored in the message

Set Methods of Message Type	
set from(author : String)	Sets the author
set id(value : String)	Sets the message identifier
set link(url : String)	Sets the link associated to the message
set location(location : Location)	Sets the geo coordinates

set media link(url : String)	Sets the url to the media
set message(message : String)	Sets the message text
set picture link(url : String)	Sets the url to the picture
set source(source : String)	Sets the source of this message
set time(time : DateTime)	Sets the time
set title(title : String)	Sets the title text
set to(author : String) : Nothing	Sets the recipient

Other Methods of Message Type	
is invalid : Boolean	Returns true if the current instance is useless
post to wall	Posts the message to the wall
share(where : String) : Nothing	Shares this message (email, sms, Facebook, social or '' to pick from a list)

C.20   Message Collection

A list of messages.

add(value : Message	Adds a Message
add many(value : Message Collection)	Adds a collection of Message items
at(index : Number) : Message	Gets the i-th Message
clear	Clears the collection
continuation : String	Gets the identifier of the next set of messages
count : Number	Gets the number of elements
index of(item : Message, start : Number) : Number	Gets the index of the first occurrence of item. Returns -1 if not found or start is out of range.
insert at(index : Number, item : Message)	Inserts a link at position index. Does nothing if index is out of range.
is invalid : Boolean	Returns true if the current instance is useless
post to wall	Displays the Messages in the wall
random : Message	Gets a random element from the collection. Returns invalid if the collection is empty.
remove(item : Message) : Boolean	Removes the first occurrence of the message. Returns true if removed.
remove at(index : Number)	Removes the message at position index
reverse	Reverses the order of the elements
set at(index : Number, value : Message)	Sets the i-th Message
set continuation(value : String)	Sets the identifier of the next set of message
sort by date	Sorts from the newest to oldest

C.21 Motion

Describes the motion of the device.

acceleration : Vector3	Gets the linear acceleration of the device, in gravitational units
gravity : Vector3	Gets the gravity vector associated with this reading
is invalid : Boolean	Returns true if the current instance is useless
pitch : Number	Gets the pitch of the attitude in degrees
post to wall	Displays the motion reading to the wall
roll : Number	Gets the roll of the attitude in degrees
rotation speed : Vector3	Gets the device rotation speed in degrees per second
time : DateTime	Gets a timestamp indicating the time at which the reading was calculated
yaw : Number	Gets the yaw of the attitude in degrees

C.22 Number

A number (possibly negative and/or fractional)

-(right : Number) : Number	Subtracts numbers
*(right : Number) : Number	Multiplies numbers
/(right : Number) : Number	Divides numbers
+(right : Number) : Number	Adds numbers
<(right : Number) : Boolean	Compares numbers for less
=(right : Number) : Boolean	Compares numbers for equality
≠(right : Number) : Boolean	Compares numbers for inequality
>(right : Number) : Boolean	Compares numbers for more
≤(right : Number) : Boolean	Compares numbers for less or equal
≥(right : Number) : Boolean	Compares numbers for more or equal
is invalid : Boolean	Returns true if the current instance is useless
post to wall	Prints the number to the wall
to character : String	Interprets a number as a unicode value and converts it to a single character string
to color : Color	Interprets the number as a ARGB (alpha, red, green, blue) color
to json : Json Object	Converts the value into a json data structure
to string : String	Converts a number to a string

C.23   Number Collection

A collection of numbers

add(item : Number)	Adds a number at the end of the collection
add many(items : Number Collection)	Adds many numbers at once
at(index : Number) : Number	Gets the number at position index. Returns invalid if index is out of range
avg : Number	Computes the average of the values
clear	Clears the numbers
contains(item : Number) : Boolean	Indicates if the collection contains the item
count : Number	Gets the number of items
index of(item : Number, start : Number) : Number	Gets the index of the first occurrence of a number. Returns -1 if not found or start is out of range.
insert at(index : Number, item : Number)	Inserts a double at position index. Does nothing if index is out of range.
is invalid : Boolean	Returns true if the current instance is useless
max : Number	Computes the maximum of the values
min : Number	Computes the minimum of the values
post to wall	Displays the numbers on the wall
random : Number	Gets a random element from the collection. Returns invalid if the collection is empty.
remove(item : Number) : Boolean	Removes the first occurrence of a number. Returns true if removed.
remove at(index : Number)	Removes the number at position index
reverse	Reverses the items
set at(index : Number, item : Number)	Sets the number at position index. Does nothing if the index is out of range.
sort	Sorts the numbers in this collection
sum : Number	Computes the sum of the values

C.24   Number Map

A map of numbers to numbers

at(index : Number) : Number	Gets the element at index. Index may be any floating-point value
avg : Number	Computes the average of the values
clear	Clears the number map
count : Number	Gets the number of elements
is invalid : Boolean	Returns true if the current instance is useless

max : Number	Computes the maximum of the values
min : Number	Computes the minimum of the values
post to wall	Displays the map in a line chart; you need to call 'update on wall' later if you want changes to be reflected
remove(index : Number)	Removes the value at a given index
set at(index : Number, value : Number)	Sets the element at index. Index may be any floating-point value
set many(numbers : Number Map)	Sets many elements at once
slice(start : Number, end : Number) : Number Map	Extracts the elements at indices between start (inclusive) and end (non-inclusive)
sum : Number	Computes the sum of the values
update on wall	Updates any display of this map

C.25   OAuth Response

OAuth 2.0 Access Token or Error.

access token : String	The access token issued by the authorization server
error : String	A single ASCII [USASCII] error code
error description : String	(Optional) A human readable error code
error uri : String	(Optional) A URI identifying a human-readable web page with information about the error, used to provide the client developer with additional information about the error.
expires in : Number	(Optional) The lifetime in seconds of the access token
is error : Boolean	Indicates if this response is an error
is expiring(lookup : Number) : Boolean	(Optional) Indicates if the token might expire within the next seconds
is invalid : Boolean	Returns true if the current instance is useless
others : String Map	(Optional) Additional key-value pairs not covered by the OAuth 2.0 specification
post to wall	Displays the response
set at(index : Number, item : Number)	Sets the number at position index. Does nothing if the index is out of range.
sort	Sorts the numbers in this collection
scope : String	(Optional) Optional if if identical to the scope requested by the client; otherwise, the scope of the access token as described by Section 3.3

C.26   Page

A page on a wall

equals(other : Page) : Boolean	Gets a value indicating if the page is equal to the other
is invalid : Boolean	Returns true if the current instance is useless

C.27   Page Button

A page button on the wall

equals(page button : Page) : Boolean	Gets a value indicating if both instances are equal
icon : String	Gets the icon name
is invalid : Boolean	Returns true if the current instance is useless
page : Page	Gets the page hosting this button
post to wall	Pushes this button on the wall
text : String	Gets the text

C.28   Page Collection

A collection of pages

at(index : Number) : Page	Gets the pages at index
count : Number	Gets the number of pages
is invalid : Boolean	Returns true if the current instance is useless
post to wall	Posts the pages on the wall

C.29   Picture

A Picture value is an image which can be displayed. The list of methods has been separated into *get methods* (which return a single property of a picture) and *other methods*.

Get Methods of Picture Type	
at(index : Number) : Color	Gets the pixel color at the given linear index
count : Number	Gets the number of pixels
date : DateTime	Gets the date and time where the picture was taken; if any

height : Number	Gets the height in pixels
location : Location	Gets the location where the picture was taken; if any.
pixel(left : Number, top : Number) : Color	Gets the color of a pixel
width : Number	Gets the width in pixels

Other Methods of Picture Type	
blend(other : Picture, left : Number, top : Number, angle : Number, opacity : Number)	Writes another picture at a given location. The opacity ranges from 0 (transparent) to 1 (opaque).
blend svg(markup : String, left : Number, top : Number, width : Number, height : Number, angle : Number)	Writes a Scalable Vector Graphics (SVG) document at a given location. By default, this action uses the viewport size provided in the SVG document when width or height are negative.
brightness(factor : Number)	Changes the brightness of the picture. Factor in [-1, 1].
clear(color : Color)	Clears the picture to a given color
clone : Picture	Returns a copy of the image
colorize(background : Color, foreground : Color, threshold : Number)	Recolors the picture with the background and foreground color, based on a color threshold between 0.0 and 1.0
contrast(factor : Number)	Changes the contrast of the picture. Factor in [-1, 1].
crop(left : Number, top : Number, width : Number, height : Number)	Crops a sub-image
desaturate	Makes the picture gray
draw ellipse(left : Number, top : Number, width : Number, height : Number, angle : Number, c : Color, thickness : Number)	Draws an elliptic border with a given color
draw line(x1 : Number, y1 : Number, x2 : Number, y2 : Number, color : Color, thickness : Number)	Draws a line between two points
draw rect(left : Number, top : Number, width : Number, height : Number, angle : Number, c : Color, thickness : Number)	Draws a rectangle border with a given color
draw text(left : Number, top : Number, text : String, font size : Number, angle : Number, color : Color)	Draws some text border with a given color and font size

fill ellipse(left : Number, top : Number, width : Number, height : Number, angle : Number, color : Color)	Fills a ellipse with a given color
fill rect(left : Number, top : Number, width : Number, height : Number, angle : Number, color : Color)	Fills a rectangle with a given color
flip horizontal	Flips the picture horizontally
flip vertical	Flips the picture vertically
invert	Inverts the red, blue and green channels
is invalid : Boolean	Returns true if the current instance is useless
is panorama : Boolean	Indicates if the picture width is greater than its height
post to wall	Displays the image to the wall; you need to call 'update on wall' later if you want changes to be reflected
resize(width : Number, height : Number)	Resizes the picture to the given size in pixels
save to library : String	Saves the picture to the 'saved pictures' album. Returns the file name.
set pixel(left : Number, top : Number, color : Color)	Sets the pixel color at a given pixel
share(where : String, message : String)	Shares this message ('' to pick from a list)
tint(color : Color)	Converts every pixel to gray and tints it with the given color.
update on wall	Refreshes the picture on the wall

C.30   Picture Album

A picture album

albums : Picture Albums	Gets the children albums
is invalid : Boolean	Returns true if the current instance is useless
name : String	Gets the name of the album
pictures : Pictures	Gets the pictures
post to wall	Displays the album to the wall

C.31   Picture Albums

A collection of picture albums

at(index : Number) : Picture Album	Gets the item at position 'index'; invalid if index is out of bounds
count : Number	Gets the number of elements in the collection
is invalid : Boolean	Returns true if the current instance is useless
post to wall	Displays the value to the wall
random : Picture Album	Gets random item; invalid if collection is empty

C.32   Pictures

A collection of pictures

at(index : Number) : Picture	Gets the item at position 'index'; invalid if index is out of bounds
count : Number	Gets the number of elements in the collection
find(name : String) : Number	Finds a picture by name and returns the index. Returns -1 if not found.
full(index : Number) : Picture	Gets the full resolution version of i-th picture
is invalid : Boolean	Returns true if the current instance is useless
post to wall	Displays the picture thumbnails to the wall
random : Picture	Gets a random item; invalid if collection is empty
thumbnail(index : Number) : Picture	Gets the thumbnail of i-th picture

C.33   Place

Attaches or uses information for a named location. The list of methods has been separate into three tables: *get methods* which access attributes of a Place, *set methods* which update or replace attributes, and *other methods*.

Get Methods of Place Type	
category : String	Gets the category of the place
id : String	Gets the identifier of this place
link : String	Gets the link associated to the message
location : Location	Gets the location of the place
name : String	Gets the name of the place
picture link : String	Gets a url to the picture
source : String	Gets the source of this place (Facebook, TouchDevelop)

Set Methods of Place Type	
set category(category : String)	Sets the category of the place
set id(id : String)	Sets the identifier of this place
set link(url : String)	Sets the link associated with the message
set location(location : Location)	Sets the location of the place
set name(name : String)	Sets the name of the place
set picture link(url : String)	Sets the url for the picture
set source(source : String)	Sets the source of this place

Other Methods of Place Type	
is invalid : Boolean	Returns true if the current instance is useless
post to wall : Nothing	Posts the place to the wall
to string : String	Converts to a string name, plus latitude and longitude

C.34   Place Collection

A collection of places

add(value : Place)	Adds a place
add many(value : Place Collection)	Adds many places at once
at(index : Number) : Place	Gets the i-th place
clear	Clears the collection
continuation : String	Gets the identifier of the next set of messages
count : Number	Gets the number of elements
index of(item : Place, start : Number) : Number	Gets the index of the first occurrence of item. Returns -1 if not found or start is out of range.
insert at(index : Number, item : Place)	Inserts a place at position index. Does nothing if index is out of range.
is invalid : Boolean	Returns true if the current instance is useless
post to wall	Posts the places on the wall
random : Place	Gets a random element from the collection. Returns invalid if the collection is empty.
remove(item : Place) : Boolean	Removes the first occurrence of a place. Returns true if removed.
remove at(index : Number)	Removes the location at position index
reverse	Reverses the order of the elements
set at(index : Number, value : Place)	Sets the i-th place
set continuation(value : String)	Sets the identifier of the next set of messages
sort by distance(loc : Location)	Sorts the places by distance to the location

C.35 Playlist

A song playlist

duration : Number	Gets the duration in seconds
is invalid : Boolean	Returns true if the current instance is useless
name : String	Gets the name of the song
play	Plays the songs in the playlist
post to wall	Displays the playlist to the wall
songs : Songs	Gets the songs

C.36 Playlists

A collection of playlists

at(index : Number) : Playlist	Gets i-th playlist
count : Number	Gets the number of playlists
is invalid : Boolean	Returns true if the current instance is useless
post to wall	Displays the value to the wall

C.37 Song

A song

album : Song Album	Gets the song album containing the song
artist : String	Gets the name of the artist
duration : Number	Gets the duration in seconds
genre : String	Gets the genre of the song
is invalid : Boolean	Returns true if the current instance is useless
name : String	Gets the name of the song
play	Plays the song
play count : Number	Gets the play count
post to wall	Displays the song on the wall
protected : Boolean	Gets a value indicating whether the song is DRM protected
rating : Number	Gets the users rating; -1 if not rated
track : Number	Gets the track number in the album

C.38   Songs

A collection of songs

at(index : Number) : Song	Gets the item at position 'index'; invalid if index is out of bounds
count : Number	Gets the number of elements in the collection
is invalid : Boolean	Returns true if the current instance is useless
play	Plays the song
post to wall	Displays the songs on the wall
random : Song	Gets random item; invalid if collection is empty

C.39   Song Album

A song album

art : Picture	Gets album art picture
artist : String	Gets the name of the artist
duration : Number	Gets the duration in seconds
genre : String	Gets the genre of the song
has art : Boolean	Indicates if the album has art
is invalid : Boolean	Returns true if the current instance is useless
name : String	Gets the name of the album
play	Plays the songs of the album
post to wall	Displays the song album on the wall
songs : Songs	Gets the songs
thumbnail : Picture	Gets the thumbnail picture

C.40   Song Albums

A collection of albums

at(index : Number) : Song Album	Gets the item at position 'index'; invalid if index is out of bounds
count : Number	Gets the number of elements in the collection
is invalid : Boolean	Returns true if the current instance is useless
post to wall	Displays the value to the wall
random : Song Album	Gets random item; invalid if collection is empty

C.41 Songs

A collection of songs.

at(index : Number) : Song	Gets the item at position 'index'; invalid if index is out of bounds
count : Number	Gets the number of elements in the collection
is invalid : Boolean	Returns true if the current instance is useless
play	Plays the song
post to wall	Displays the songs on the wall
random : Song	Gets random item; invalid if collection is empty

C.42 Sound

A sound effect

duration : Number	Gets the duration in seconds
is invalid : Boolean	Returns true if the current instance is useless
pan : Number	Gets the panning, ranging from -1.0 (full left) to 1.0 (full right)
pitch : Number	Gets the pitch adjustment, ranging from -1 (down one octave) to 1 (up one octave)
play	Plays the sound effect
play special(volume : Number, pitch : Number, pan : Number)	Plays the song with different volume (0 to 1), pitch (-1 to 1) and pan (-1 to 1)
post to wall	Displays a player on the wall
set pan(pan : Number)	Sets the panning, ranging from -1.0 (full left) to 1.0 (full right)
set pitch(pitch : Number)	Sets the pitch adjustment, ranging from -1 (down one octave) to 1 (up one octave)
set volume(v : Number)	Sets the volume from 0 (silent) to 1 (full volume)
volume : Number	Gets the volume from 0 (silent) to 1 (full volume)

C.43 Sprite

A sprite is a graphical object which can be displayed on a Board instance. The list of methods of the Sprite type has been separated into get methods (which return a single attribute), *set methods* (which assign or update an attribute), and *other methods*.

Get Methods of Sprite Type	
acceleration x : Number	Gets the acceleration along x in pixels/sec^2
acceleration y : Number	Gets the acceleration along y in pixels/sec^2
angle : Number	Gets the angle of the sprite in degrees
angular speed : Number	Gets the rotation speed in degrees/sec
color : Color	Gets the sprite color
elasticity : Number	Gets the sprite elasticity as a fraction of speed preservation per bounce (0-1)
friction : Number	Gets the fraction of speed loss between 0 and 1
height : Number	Gets the height in pixels
location : Location	Gets the geo location assigned to the sprite
mass : Number	Gets the mass
opacity : Number	Gets the opacity (between 0 transparent and 1 opaque)
picture : Picture	Gets the picture on a picture sprite (if it is a picture sprite)
speed x : Number	Gets the speed along x in pixels/sec
speed y : Number	Gets the speed along y in pixels/sec
text : String	The text on a text sprite (if it is a text sprite)
width : Number	Gets the width in pixels
x : Number	Gets the x position in pixels
y : Number	Gets the y position in pixels
z index : Number	Gets the z-index of the sprite

Set Methods of Sprite Type	
set acceleration(vx : Number, vy : Number)	Sets the acceleration in pixels/sec^2
set acceleration x(vx : Number)	Sets the x acceleration in pixels/sec^2
set acceleration y(vy : Number)	Sets the y acceleration in pixels/sec^2
set angle(angle : Number)	Sets the angle of the sprite in degrees
set angular speed(speed : Number)	Sets the rotation speed in degrees/sec
set clip(left : Number, top : Number, width : Number, height : Number)	Sets the clipping area for an image sprite (if it is an image sprite)
set elasticity(elasticity : Number)	Sets the sprite elasticity as a fraction of speed preservation per bounce (0-1)
set friction(friction : Number)	Sets the friction to a fraction of speed loss between 0 and 1
set height(height : Number)	Sets the height in pixels
set location(location : Location)	Sets the geo location of the sprite
set mass(mass : Number)	Sets the sprite mass
set opacity(opacity : Number)	Sets the sprite opacity (between 0 transparent and 1 opaque)

Set Methods of Sprite Type	
set picture(pic : Picture) : Nothing	Updates picture on a picture sprite (if it is a picture sprite)
set pos(x : Number, y : Number)	Sets the position in pixels
set speed(vx : Number, vy : Number)	Sets the speed in pixels/sec
set speed x(vx : Number)	Sets the x speed in pixels/sec
set speed y(vy : Number)	Sets the y speed in pixels/sec
set text(text : String)	Updates text on a text sprite (if it is a text sprite)
set width(width : Number)	Sets the width in pixels
set x(x : Number)	Sets the x position in pixels
set y(y : Number) : Nothing	Sets the y position in pixels
set z index(zindex : Number)	Sets the z-index of the sprite
speed towards(other : Sprite, magnitude : Number)	Sets sprite speed direction towards other sprite with given magnitude

Other Methods of Sprite Type	
delete	Delete sprite
equals(other : Sprite) : Boolean	Are these the same sprite?
hide	Hide the sprite
is invalid : Boolean	Returns true if the current instance is useless
is visible : Boolean	Returns true if sprite is not hidden
move(delta x : Number, delta y : Number)	Moves sprite
move clip(x : Number, y : Number)	Moves the clipping area and wraps around the image if needed (if it is an image sprite)
move towards(other : Sprite, fraction : Number)	Moves sprite towards other sprite
overlap with(sprites : Sprite Set) : Sprite Set	Returns the subset of sprites in the given set that overlap with sprite
overlaps with(other : Sprite) : Boolean	Do the sprites overlap?
show	Show the sprite

C.44 Sprite Set

A collection of sprites. Unlike the other collection types, a Sprite Set does not allow duplicate items, and the items in the set are ordered.

add(sprite : Sprite) : Boolean	Add sprite to set. Returns true if sprite was not already in set.

add from(old set : Sprite Set, sprite : Sprite) : Boolean	Add sprite to set and remove from old set. Returns true if sprite was in old set and not in new set.
at(index : Number) : Sprite	Return sprite at given index
clear	Removes all sprites from the set
contains(sprite : Sprite) : Boolean	Returns true if sprite is in set
count : Number	Returns the number of sprites in the set
index of(sprite : Sprite) : Number	Returns index of sprite in this set or -1 if not in set
is invalid : Boolean	Returns true if the current instance is useless
remove(sprite : Sprite) : Boolean	Remove sprite from set. Returns true if sprite was in set
remove first : Sprite	Remove sprite that was added to set first

C.45   String

A piece of text.

‖(right : String) : String	Concatenates two pieces of text
at(index : Number) : String	Gets the character at a specified index
compare(other : String) : Number	Compares two pieces of text
concat(other : String) : String	Concatenates two pieces of text
contains(value : String) : Boolean	Returns a value indicating if the second string is contained
copy to clipboard	Stores text in the clipboard
count : Number	Returns the number of characters
ends with(value : String) : Boolean	Determines whether the ending matches the specified string
equals(other : String) : Boolean	Checks if two strings are the same
index of(value : String, start : Number) : Number	Returns the index of the first occurrence if found starting at a given position
insert(start : Number, value : String) : String	Inserts a string at a given position
is empty : Boolean	Indicates if the string is empty
is invalid : Boolean	Returns true if the current instance is useless
is match regex(pattern : String) : Boolean	Indicates if the string matches a regular expression
last index of(value : String, start : Number) : Number	Returns the index of the last occurrence if found starting at a given position
matches(pattern : String) : String Collection	Gets the strings matching the regex expression (pattern)
post to wall	Displays string on the wall
remove(start : Number) : String	Returns all character from a string starting at a given index

replace(old : String, new : String) : String	Returns a given string with a replacement
replace regex(pattern : String, replace : String) : String	Replace every match of the regex according to the replacement string
share(network : String)	Shares the string (email, sms, Facebook, social or " to pick from a list)
split(separator : String) : String Collection	Returns a string collection that contains the substrings in this string that are delimited by elements of a specified string
starts with(value : String) : Boolean	Determines whether the beginning matches the specified string
substring(start : Number, length : Number) : String	Returns a substring given a start index and a length
to boolean : Boolean	Parses the string as a boolean
to color : Color	Parses the string as a color
to datetime : DateTime	Parses the string as a date and time
to json : Json Object	Converts the value into a json data structure
to location : Location	Parses the string as a geo coordinate
to lower case : String	Returns a copy of this string converted to lowercase, using the casing rules of the current culture
to number : Number	Parses the string as a number
to time : Number	Parses the string as a time (12:30:12) and returns the number of seconds
to unicode : Number	Converts a single character string into its unicode number
to upper case : String	Returns a copy of this string converted to uppercase, using the casing rules of the current culture
trim(chars : String) : String	Removes all leading and trailing occurrences of a set of characters specified in a string from the current string
trim end(chars : String) : String	Removes all trailing occurrences of a set of characters specified in a string from the current string
trim start(chars : String) : String	Removes all leading occurrences of a set of characters specified in a string from the current string

C.46   String Collection

A collection of strings

add(item : String)	Adds a string
add many(items : String Collection)	Adds many strings at once
at(index : Number) : String	Gets the string at position index. Returns invalid if index is out of range.
clear	Clears the strings
contains(item : String) : Boolean	Indicates if the collection contains the item
count : Number	Gets the number of strings
index of(item : String, start : Number) : Number	Gets index of the first occurrence of a string. Returns -1 if not found or start is out of range.
insert at(index : Number, item : String) : Nothing	Inserts a string at position index. Does nothing if index is out of range.
is invalid : Boolean	Returns true if the current instance is useless
join(separator : String) : String	Concatenates separator and items into a string
post to wall	Displays the string on the wall
random : String	Gets a random element from the collection. Returns invalid if the collection is empty.
remove(item : String) : Boolean	Removes the first occurrence of a string. Returns true if removed.
remove at(index : Number) : Nothing	Removes the string at position index
reverse	Reverses the items
set at(index : Number, item : String)	Sets the string at position index. Does nothing if the index is out of range.
sort	Sorts the strings in this collection

C.47   String Map

A map from strings to strings

at(key : String) : String	Gets the value at a given key; invalid if not found
clear	Clears the values from the map
count : Number	Gets the number of elements in the map
is invalid : Boolean	Returns true if the current instance is useless
keys : String Collection	Gets the keys in the map
post to wall	Displays the list of key,value pairs in a table
remove(key : String)	Removes the value at a given key
set at(key : String, value : String) : Nothing	Sets the value at a given key; invalid if not found
set many(other : String Map) :	Sets many elements at once

Nothing	

C.48   TextBox

A text box

background : Color	Gets the background color
border : Color	Gets the border color
font size : Number	Gets the font size
foreground : Color	Gets the foreground color
icon : Picture	Gets the icon picture (max 173x173)
is invalid : Boolean	Returns true if current instance is useless
post to wall	Posts the textbox to the wall
set background(color : Color)	Sets the background color
set border(color : Color)	Sets the border color
set font size(size: Number)	Sets font size (small = 14, normal = 15, medium = 17, medium large = 19, large = 24, extra large = 32, extra extra large = 54, huge = 140
set foreground(color : Color)	Sets the foreground color
set icon(pic : Picture)	Sets the icon picture (max 96 x 96)
set text(text : String)	Sets the text
text : String	Gets the text

C.49   Vector3

A 3D vector

add(other : Vector3) : Vector3	Adds a vector
clamp(min : Vector3, max : Vector3) : Vector3	Restricts the vector in the specified range
cross(other : Vector3) : Vector3	Calculates the cross product with the other vector
distance(other : Vector3) : Number	Gets the distance between the two vectors
is invalid : Boolean	Returns true if the current instance is useless
length : Number	Gets the length of the vector
linear interpolation(other : Vector3, amount : Number) : Vector3	Linear interpolation between two vectors
multiply(other : Vector3) : Vector3	Multiplies component-wise with a vector

negate : Vector3	Returns a vector pointing in the opposite direction
normalize : Vector3	Returns a vector of one unit pointing in the same direction as the original vector
post to wall	Displays the vector on the wall
scale(scalar : Number) : Vector3	Multiplies with a scaling factor
subtract(other : Vector3) : Vector3	Subtracts another vector
to string : String	Turns the vector into a string
x : Number	Gets the x-component
y : Number	Gets the y-component
z : Number	Gets the z-component

C.50   Web Request

An HTTP web request

equals(other : Web Request) : Boolean	Indicates if both requests are the same instance
header(name : String) : String	Gets the value of a given header
header names : String Collection	Gets the names of the headers
is invalid : Boolean	Returns true if the current instance is useless
method : String	Determines whether it was a 'get' or a 'post'
on response received(handler : Web Response Action)	Set what happens whenever the response comes back from 'send async'
post to wall	Displays the request on the wall
send : Web Response	Performs the request synchronously
set accept(type : String)	Sets the Accept header type ('text/xml' for XML, 'application/json' for JSON)
set compress(value : Boolean)	Compresses the request content with gzip and sets the Content-Encoding header
set content(content : String)	Sets the content of a 'post' request
set content as form(form : Form Builder)	Sets the content as multipart/form-data
set content as json(json : Json Object)	Sets the content of a 'post' request as the JSON tree
set content as picture(picture : Picture, quality : Number)	Sets the content of a 'post' request as a JPEG encoded image. Quality from 0 (worse) to 1 (best).
set content as xml(xml : Xml Object)	Sets the content of a 'post' request as the XML tree
set credentials(name : String, password : String)	Sets the name and password for basic authentication. Requires an HTTPS URL, empty string clears.
set header(name : String, value : String)	Sets an HTML header value. An empty string clears the value

set method(method : String)	Sets the method as 'get' or 'post'. Default value is 'get'
set url(url : String)	Sets the url of the request. Must be a valid internet address.
url : String	Gets the url of the request

C.51   Web Response

An HTTP web response

content : String	Reads the response body as a string
content as json : Json Object	Reads the response body as a JSON tree
content as picture : Picture	Reads the response body as a picture
content as sound : Sound	Reads the response body as a wave sound
content as xml : Xml Object	Reads the response body as a XML tree
header(name : String) : String	Gets the value of a given header
header names : String Collection	Gets the names of the headers
is invalid : Boolean	Returns true if the current instance is useless
post to wall	Displays the response to the wall
request : Web Request	Gets the request associated to this response
status code : Number	Gets the HTTP Status code of the request if any

C.52   Xml Object

An xml element or collection of elements.

at(index : Number) : Xml Object	Gets the i-th child element in the collection
attr(name : String) : String	Gets the value of the attribute
attr names : String Collection	Gets the list of attribute names
child(name : String) : Xml Object	Gets a first child element matching the fully qualified name
children(name : String) : Xml Object	Gets a collection of child element matching the fully qualified name
count : Number	Gets the number of child element
create name(local name : String, namespace uri : String) : String	Creates a qualified full name from the namespace and local name
is element : Boolean	Indicates if this instance is an element or a filtered collection
is invalid : Boolean	Returns true if the current instance is useless
local name : String	Gets the local name of this element
name : String	Gets the full name of this element

namespace : String	Gets the namespace of this element
post to wall	Display the xml content on the wall
to string : String	Gets an xml string
value : String	Gets the concatenated text contents of this element

Appendix D
Platform Capabilities

Resources (services) provided by TouchDevelop are dependent on the capabilities of a particular platforms. Some methods of some datatypes may only be available on certain devices. They will not be listed by the TouchDevelop editor unless the target platform is set appropriately in the script properties.[1]

D.1   Supported Browsers

The WebApp version of TouchDevelop requires the versions of browsers shown in the table below.

Platform	Browser
PC, Mac, Linux	Internet Explorer 10, Safari 6+, Chrome 22+, Firefox 16+
iPad, iPhone, iPod Touch	Mobile Safari on iOS 6+
Android	Chrome 18+

D.2   General Features

Support for these general characteristics of the TouchDevelop system is provided by the WebApp for all supported platform/browser combinations and by the TouchDevelop app v2.11 for Windows Phones:

- The full TouchDevelop scripting language
- Execution of TouchDevelop scripts
- Editing of TouchDevelop scripts

---

[1] This appendix reproduces material found on the TouchDevelop website at https://www.touchdevelop.com/platforms

- Offline editing and script execution
- Ability to login with a Microsoft, Facebook or Google account

These sections of a TouchDevelop script may be used in a script that is to be executed in a browser but cannot be used yet in a script to be run on the Windows phone:

- Pages and Boxes (see Chapter 10)
- Libraries making use of Records (see Chapter 2)

D.3   Supported Sensors and Devices

Even if a tablet or computer possesses sensors and devices that a TouchDevelop script could normally utilize, the operating system may disallow access, or make access difficult, for programs running in a browser. The table below shows the current status of which sensors and devices may be accessed on which platform. (Note: all these sensors and devices are supported on a Windows phone.)

Sensor/Device	Support Status
Accelerometer	Available for iPad, iPhone, iPod Touch. Emulated on PC, Mac, Linux by tracking mouse (or finger touch) movements. Emulated on Android by tracking device orientation; the acceleration vector has a fixed magnitude.
Camera	Available with Chrome browser on PC, Mac, Linux and Android.
Compass	Available for iPad, iPhone, iPod Touch and Android.
Gyroscope	Available for iPad, iPhone, iPod.
Microphone	Planned to be available for iPad, iPhone, iPod and Android.
Motion	Planned to be available for iPad, iPhone, iPod and Android.
Phone	Available if the device has phone call capability or if Lync or Skype is installed.
Orientation	Planned to be available for iPad, iPhone, iPod and Android.

D.4   Support for Services/Resources·

With one exception all the resources (or services) provided by the TouchDevelop API and listed in Appendix B are available on the Windows Phone. That exception is the language translation services provided by Project Hawaii. They are temporarily unavailable.

The resources listed in the table below have limited support or no support on the PC, Mac, iPad, iPhone, iPod Touch and Android platforms.

Resource	Support Status
social/calendar	No support for accessing a user's calendar through the social resource
social/contacts	No support for accessing contacts through the social resource
media/songs	No support for accessing songs or song albums through the media resource
media/pictures	No support for accessing pictures or picture albums through the media resource

D.5   Support for Created Apps

A created app refers to an app which has been exported to the Windows Phone Store or to the Windows Store (which holds apps for the Surface tablet and PCs which run the Windows 8 operating system).

D.5.1   Apps for Windows Phone Store

The scripts cannot make use of boxes and pages or libraries.

The scripts cannot make use of the language translation services provided by Project Hawaii.

D.5.2   Apps for Windows Store

The script cannot make use of a gyroscope or microphone or motion sensors or orientation sensors, but future support for these devices is planned.

Appendix E
TouchDevelop Editor on a Windows Phone

This appendix provides a worked example of using the TouchDevelop editor on a Windows phone. It does not cover all the editor's features. Some experimentation is suggested for gaining familiarity with the editor.

E.1   The sample program

The script to be entered is shown in Figure A-1. It is published under the name *rotor* with code name /cqxk.

E.2   The back button, undo and mistakes

The phone has three buttons below the touch sensitive screen. The important button used frequently in editing a script is the *phone back button*. Its main purpose is to return the screen to a previous state. It is often useful for recovering from a mistake. If, for example, the bing button is accidentally touched in the middle of an editing session and the bing search engine comes up, the back button will exit from bing and return to the editor.

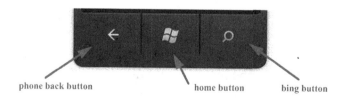

phone back button   home button   bing button

While editing, there is an *undo button* provided on the top row of every edit menu. When it is not dimmed, tapping that undo button will do exactly what it says.

Figure A-1: The rotor program /cqxk

```
action main(speed: Number)
    ⊟rate := speed
    ⊟bd := media → create board(480)
    var sprite := ⊟bd → create rectangle(360, 60)
    if speed > 10 then
        sprite → set color(colors → red)
    else
        sprite → set color(colors → blue)
    ⊟bd → post to wall

// global data variables
var rate : Number
var bd : Board

event gameloop( )
    var sprite := ⊟bd → at(0)
    var x := sprite → angle + ⊟rate
    sprite → set angle(x)
    ⊟bd → update on wall
```

E.3   The editing example

The screen contents change many times as the editing steps detailed below are followed. For space reasons, only a selection of the screenshots can be included in this chapter.

Getting started

1. Start TouchDevelop.
2. Tap the + button at the bottom. [Figure A-2a]
3. Rename the script to rotor.
4. See all the script components. [Figure A-2b]. Tap the identifier main.
5. See the initial main action with its default body.
6. Tap anywhere on the statement inside the action.
7. Tap the cut button in the edit menu [Figure A-2c]
8. Tap anywhere in the top line on the screen (which begins with the keyword action).
9. Tap the edit button. [Figure A-2d]

10. Tap the word params or drag the screen left to select params. (The params name is called a *pivot*; there are several pivots which can be selected, showing different features of the action.)
11. Tap the '+' button at the bottom. [Figure A-2e]
12. Tap the default parameter name x1 and enter the name speed as its replacement. [Figure A-2f]
13. Tap the phone back button.

Figure A-2: Getting started screenshots

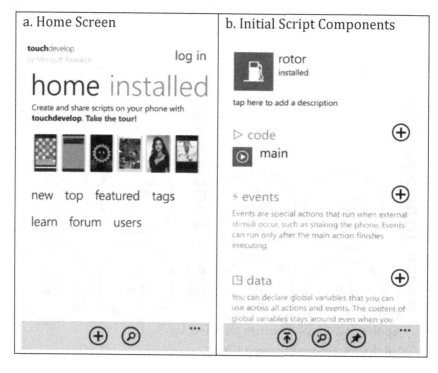

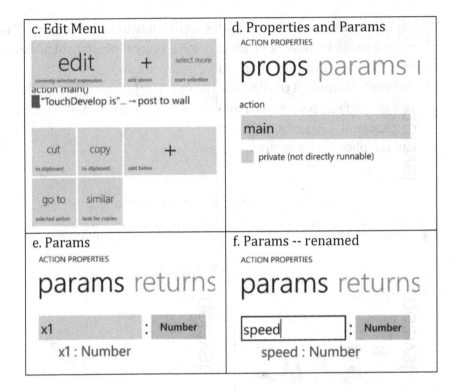

The second line of code in the main action

1. Tap in the white space below the first line of code and tap the + (add expression) button.
2. Tap the row 2, col 3 button (labeled *and or* ...); then select ':='.
3. Tap the button labeled media, this refers to the media resource.
4. Tap create board, this refers to one of the media methods.
5. Tap the row 2, col 1 button (labeled 1 2 3 ...).
6. Tap the backspace button 3 times.
7. Tap the 4 8 and 0 buttons in sequence to enter 480.
8. Tap the '....' variable name, and rename it to bd, tapping the phone back button afterwards.
9. Tap the bd variable name and tap the promote to ⊞data button.

Figure A-3: Editing the first line

a. Edit menu	b. Inserting an element

a. Edit menu

if	for each	for	while
condition is true then	item in collection	numbers up to repeat	is true repeat

action main(speed : Number)
▪ do nothing

comment	var	command
explain your code	new variable	perform a task

paste	search
from clipboard	explore commands

b. Inserting an element

←	→	↶	⌫
move cursor	move cursor	undo	backspace

1 2 3 ·	+ - · /	and or not xor	go and come
4 5 6	< ≤ ≥ >	not true	
7 8 9 0	= ≠ ( )		
			strings, art

time	senses	speed	collections
service	service	local Number	collections

colors	social	🔍	▶▶
service	service	there's more	next suggestions

c. Named operators	d. Promote to global data

c. Named operators

←	→	↶	⌫
move cursor	move cursor	undo	backspace

and	or	not	post to wall

true	false		‖
			concatenate strings

≔		/	
assignment			

d. Promote to global data

store the current expression here. Use [rename] button
below to rename   more...

←	→	↶	⌫
move cursor	move cursor	undo	backspace

			strings, art

cut	copy	paste	rename

promote to ⊞data		🔍	▶▶
to global var		there's more	next suggestions

The third line of code in the main action

1. Tap in the white space below the last line of code, tap the '+' (add expression) button.
2. Tap the ⊞data button and tap the bd button to insert this global variable.
3. Tap the bottom right button labeled next suggestions, tap a few more times until create rectangle appears on a button. Tap it.
4. Tap the row 2, col 1 button (1 2 3 ...), and then edit the 200 to turn it into 360.
5. Using the move cursor buttons, move the cursor between the 2 and 0

digits, then replace the 2 with 6.

6. Oops, we wanted to save the whole expression in a variable; drag across the whole line of code to highlight it. The menu of choices has changed; tap the extract to var button.

7. Tap the phone back button to see what happened.

8. Tap that last line of code (consisting of just the variable sprite), and tap the cut button.

Starting the if statement

1. Tap the + button at the bottom of the screen.
2. Tap the button labeled if.
3. Tap the button labeled speed.
4. Tap the row 2, col 2 button (labeled + - ...).
5. Tap the > button.
6. Tap the row 2, col 1 button (labeled 1 2 3 ...), and tap 1 and tap 0 so that the number 10 is produced.

The 'then' clause of the if statement

1. Tap in white space below the line of code beginning with the if keyword; tap '+' (add expression).
2. Tap the button labeled sprite, hit the next suggestions button several times until set color appears as a button; tap it.
3. Tap the identifier random in the supplied default parameter value, and tap the backspace button to delete the identifier.
4. Tap next suggestions until red appears as a choice; tap it.
5. The then clause is finished (we would tap the white below if there's another statement to add to the clause); tap the phone back button.

The else clause of the if statement

1. Tap the keyword else, then tap '+' (add below); then tap the button labeled command.
2. Enter the line of code sprite → set color(colors → blue) in a similar manner to steps 2-4 under the 'then clause' heading; tap the phone back button.

The last statement of the main action

1. Tap the keyword if to select the whole if statement; tap '+' add below;

tap the command button.

2. Select ▣data, select bd; tap next suggestions to find the post to wall method and tap it.

3. Tap the phone back button, and we have the entire main action completed.

4. Tap the phone back button again; we can see the main action plus one of the two global data items.

The gameloop event

1. Tap the '+' button to the right of the word *events*.

2. Tap the gameloop identifier.

3. Tap the '+' button at the bottom of the screen to add code; tap the command button.

4. Enter the line of code var sprite := ▣bd → at(0) using steps similar to steps 2-6 under the *'third line of code'* heading above.

5. Enter the line of code var x := sprite → angle + ▣rate similarly.

6. Enter the line sprite → set angle(x) similarly to steps 2-4 under the *'then clause'* heading.

7. Enter the line ▣bd → update on wall.

8. Tap the phone back button to go back to the script's components.

Trying out the script

1. Tap the triangle inside the square to the left of the name main to run the script.

2. Enter a value (say 10) for speed and tap go. [Figure A-4a]

3. Tap the phone back button to stop execution. [Figure A-4b]

4. Tap the phone back button again to return to the script components.

E.4　Additional steps

Revising the script

If the script does not behave as expected or needs improvement, it is easy to go back and edit the code. On the screen where the script components are listed, just tap the name of the action or the name of the event to open up the code for that action or event.

Figure A-4: Running the script

| a. Starting the script | b. View while running |

After scrolling, if necessary, to the line of code which is to be changed or where new code is to be inserted, tap that line. The edit menu then provides the choices of editing that line, deleting that line (the cut button), inserting above or inserting below.

If an existing line of code is being edited, the part to be changed can be tapped, the part can be deleted, and new program elements can be inserted. The edit menu choices should be intuitive.

Publishing the script

If the code is something that is worth sharing with others, or if it is to be saved to permanent storage on a web server, the script can be published. Tapping the upward pointing arrow at the bottom begins the process.

A Windows Live ID or Facebook ID is needed before the script can be published. There is a choice of keeping the script *hidden* or making it *visible*. If it is marked as visible, then anyone searching the TouchDevelop website for an example of a particular language feature or script feature may be directed to this script. It can also appear in lists of new scripts, or featured scripts. If it is marked as hidden, then it will not show up in such searches (but anyone knowing the codename for the script can still access it).

Missing buttons?

There are 23 different resources, and a resource or datatype can provide a large number of methods. A script can contain a very large number of variables. The editor does not necessarily provide a button for every one of the valid choices.

If a resource, variable or method is not provided on a button, there is a catch-all button which can be used. This is the button showing a magnifying glass icon and labeled "there's more". It can be seen in the bottom row of both Figure B.3b and Figure B.3d. Tapping this button brings up a scrollable and searchable list of all the valid choices. Scrolling through the list and tapping the desired item will insert it into the script. Alternatively entering the first few characters of the name will cause the list to jump to the desired point.

E.5   Refactoring code into a new action

A group of consecutive statements inside an action or event is first selected. To do this, select the first line in the sequence. When the edit menu appears, the button labeled select more should be tapped. Then the code in the center window can be dragged to extend the selection from one statement to multiple statements.

Once all the statements have been selected (as indicated by the solid bar shown to the left of the selection), the button labeled extract should be tapped. This causes the selected statements to be deleted from the current action, inserted into a newly created action, and replaced by a call to the new action. TouchDevelop asks for a name for this new action. The action is given parameters so that the extracted code will work without any further editing being needed.

Index